MONEY SMART TEENS:
WHAT THEY DON'T TEACH IN SCHOOL

THE STRATEGIC GUIDE TO LEARNING HOW TO SAVE,
SPEND, AND GROW WEALTH WITHOUT FEELING OVERWHELMED

SKYLAR HAYES

CONTENTS

INTRODUCTION

When Liam got his first summer job at sixteen, he was excited to finally earn his own money. His plan was to save up for a car. But week after week, his paycheck disappeared faster than expected— and he was left wondering where it all went. Sound familiar? If you've ever asked yourself that same question, you're not alone.

More than half of teens—54 percent, according to a study by Junior Achievement and Citizens—say they feel unprepared to handle their financial futures. That's a big deal. And it's exactly why this book exists.

I know how that feels. When I was younger, no one really taught me how to manage money. I made plenty of mistakes and had to learn the hard way. That's why I created this guide—to give you what I wish I had: real-world advice, clear steps, and a little encouragement to help you build confidence with money from the start.

Money Smarts for Teens is here to help you take charge of your money and give you the tools to build a strong financial foundation—starting now. Whether you're saving for your first phone, a laptop for school, college costs, or your first apartment, you'll find simple strategies that actually work. There are no lectures or confusing finance talk—just real-world advice, examples that make sense, and smart tips you can start using right away. You'll learn how to manage your money, avoid common mistakes, and make choices that set you up for the future you want.

We'll talk about budgeting, saving, credit, investing, and more— but we won't stop there. Each chapter includes a Money Smarts Challenge—an easy, hands-on way to apply what you've learned and build confidence as you go. You'll also get stories from teens who've faced money struggles and figured it out. Their wins (and mistakes) will show you what's possible and remind you that no one starts off knowing everything. Along the way, we'll cover the basics, like how to track your spending and build a budget, and also take a look at newer topics, like side hustles, the gig economy, and how cryptocurrency fits into the mix. This book is designed for you—for the world you're living in now.

By the end, you'll walk away with a solid action plan and real-life skills that help you save smarter, spend wisely, and feel more confident with your money. More importantly, you'll feel capable and ready. Money won't be something that stresses you out or catches you off guard. You'll know how to make it work for you.

You don't have to be perfect or have everything figured out. But now's a great time to start building habits that will pay off later— literally. Let's start!

1

MONEY 101: WHAT SCHOOL

DOESN'T TEACH YOU

ABOUT CASH

When Emma stood at the mall with her friends, she faced a choice that most teens know well: spend her cash on those cool new sneakers or keep saving for tickets to the summer music festival. Sound familiar? For a lot of people your age, dealing with money can feel overwhelming, tedious, or just plain confusing. But here's the thing: Handling your cash doesn't have to be complicated. If you pick up a few simple money habits now, you'll build the confidence and freedom to make choices that'll help you for years down the road.

Here's why this stuff matters: Young Americans owe more than $1 trillion in debt, and 70 percent of millennials live paycheck to paycheck (United Way of the National Capital Area 2023). Those numbers might seem scary, but they're exactly why starting early —even with small steps—can make a difference.

Before you can make smart choices with your cash, you need to get comfortable with the basics. Learning common money terms isn't about memorizing jargon—it's about knowing what's happening with your money so you can avoid mistakes and plan

for the stuff you care about. Let's start with the words you'll hear most often.

TALK THE TALK

Every day, when you pull cash from an ATM, tap your card to buy a soda, or use your phone to send money to friends, you're already dealing with money terms and concepts. Let's break down some of the most important ones clearly so you're confident about what they mean.

First up is the ATM—or Automated Teller Machine. You've probably used one plenty of times without even thinking about it. An ATM is a handy machine that lets you access your money whenever you need it. But remember: Some ATMs charge fees if they don't belong to your bank. Knowing this helps you avoid unnecessary charges and keeps your cash in your pocket where it belongs.

Another area that confuses a lot of teens is the difference between debit cards and credit cards. They look pretty similar, and you can use both to buy stuff online or at stores. But there's a big difference in how they work. With a debit card, every purchase immediately comes from the money in your bank account. That means you only spend what's already yours, which keeps you from going into debt. A credit card, however, lets you borrow money up to a specific limit, which you'll have to repay. If you don't pay it back on time, interest charges can add up fast. With this knowledge, you can make choices that match your budget and keep you out of financial trouble.

Speaking of interest—let's clear that up, too. Interest is the extra money added to either savings or borrowed money. If you borrow money, like with a credit card or a loan, interest is the extra you pay for the privilege of borrowing. On the bright side, interest can

also work for you. When you save money in certain types of accounts, the bank pays you interest as a reward. Getting yourself familiar with interest helps you choose wisely when deciding how to borrow money or where to put your savings, which means you're always one step ahead.

Let's look at a quick example to put this all together. Let's say you're buying a ticket to see your favorite band online. You'll probably have the option to pay with debit or credit. Now, you decide whether to use the money you already have (debit) or borrow money to pay later (credit). Another scenario is when you're out with friends and split a restaurant bill. Since you now know how cards and transactions work, you will not be spending more than planned, and you will protect your budget.

The cool thing is, once you start speaking money confidently, it can help you in surprising ways, like negotiating a better pay rate for your part-time job or understanding what your bank statements really mean. Suddenly, these tasks become simple, and you'll feel capable of handling more money situations on your own.

Let's take a look at more terms. According to the First Commonwealth Federal Credit Union (n.d.), below are the financial terms every teen should know:

APR (Annual Percentage Rate): A number that tells you how much interest you'll pay if you borrow money over one year or how much you'll earn if you invest money— but it doesn't include interest on interest.

APY (Annual Percentage Yield): Similar to APR but better because it includes interest on top of interest, helping your money grow even faster.

Compounding Interest: The interest you earn not only on your initial savings or investments but also on the interest you've

already earned. Think of it as interest building upon itself, helping your money multiply faster. **Budget:** A clear plan that helps you decide how much money you'll spend, save, or use for specific goals, helping you stay on track with your finances.

- **Debt:** Money you've borrowed and must repay. Debt is like an IOU and often includes interest charges. **Credit:** The ability to
- buy something now but pay for it later. It's

essentially borrowed money you're responsible for paying back.

Direct Deposit: A quick, electronic way of getting paid directly into your bank account, skipping the hassle of paper checks.

Investment: Using money to buy something—like stocks, property, or other assets—that you expect to grow in value and make you more money over time.

Loan: Money you borrow, often from a bank, that you must pay back, usually with interest. Examples include student loans, car loans, or home loans.

Mobile Banking: Using your smartphone or tablet to handle your banking needs, like checking your balance, sending money, or managing your accounts anytime, anywhere.

Mobile Deposit: Using your phone's camera through a banking app to deposit a check electronically, saving you a trip to the bank or ATM.

Routing Number: A unique nine-digit code identifying your bank. You'll usually need it when setting up direct deposits or making electronic payments.

Saving: Putting money aside regularly instead of spending

it immediately, preparing for bigger purchases or unexpected costs down the line.

Stop Payment: Asking your bank to prevent a check or payment from being processed. This is useful if a check gets lost or you accidentally send money to the wrong person.

Wire Transfer: Electronically sending money quickly and safely to someone else, either across the country or around the world.

Learning these words might feel a little overwhelming, so try creating your own "Money Word of the Day" challenge with friends. Each day, pick a term, talk about what it means, and use it in conversation. You could even make a game of it—quiz each other, keep score, and see who knows the most by the end of the week.

Flashcards or quick digital quizzes on your phone can help these terms stick easily. Short, frequent practice makes learning simple.

Think back to Emma at the mall. Understanding terms like budgeting, credit, debt, and saving would have made her decision easier. She'd quickly realize that buying those sneakers on a credit card might lead to interest charges later, meaning less money available for the music festival she really cares about.

Now, it's your turn. Knowing these terms helps you handle everyday decisions confidently. Whether you're getting your first paycheck from a part-time job, splitting pizza with friends, or deciding whether you can afford a new phone, you'll be ready with the knowledge you need.

And remember—financial literacy is simply about learning enough to make smart, stress-free decisions. Soon, you'll see just how great it feels to understand exactly where your money is going and how to make it work for you.

Now, let's keep moving forward and build on these basics. You've already taken the first big step toward becoming money-smart.

IT'S ALL IN YOUR HEAD

Have you ever wondered why some people seem confident about their money while others constantly feel stressed about it? It might surprise you, but managing money is also about your mindset. Your mindset is simply how you think and feel about money. The way you think can change your entire financial future, either helping you feel relaxed or causing stress and worry.

Think about this scenario: Your friend Selena got paid from a weekend job and immediately bought new clothes and games, while your other friend Jin put most of his paycheck into savings for a trip next summer. Both friends handled their money differently because of how they think about money.

There are two common mindsets teens often have about money: scarcity and abundance.

A scarcity mindset means you always worry there won't be enough money. You feel anxious about spending anything, and you are always afraid of running out. This mindset can make you hold onto every dollar tightly, never allowing yourself to enjoy your money or invest in things that could make your life better. For example, Jake always skips social events or avoids buying snacks, even though he has enough money. He's constantly worried he won't have enough cash for something important later. He ends up missing out on fun experiences because he's afraid of spending.

On the other hand, an abundance mindset means believing there are plenty of opportunities to earn and manage money wisely. No, it doesn't mean spending recklessly, but instead seeing money as a useful tool rather than something to fear. Take Annie: She set aside cash from her allowance and birthday gifts all year to go to a music festival with friends. She didn't have unlimited funds but focused on what she could do. By tracking her spending and prioritizing what mattered most, she enjoyed the trip and had cash left for fun extras.

So, how do we change our mindset about money? Simple. Below are a few ideas from Ramsey Solutions (Cruze 2025).

Fill Your Head with Good Stuff

Books are like cheat codes for life. They let you borrow wisdom from folks who've already made—and fixed—money mistakes. For example, *The Total Money Makeover* by Dave Ramsey breaks down how to ditch debt, while *The Power of Habit* by Charles Duhigg explains why we overspend on stuff we don't need. Pick one book a month (even audiobooks count!) and jot down one idea you'll try. ***Reflect on Your Money Roots***

Your childhood sneaks into your money habits more than you think. Maybe your parents argued about bills, so now you avoid checking your bank account. Or perhaps they never talked about money at all, leaving you clueless. Grab a journal and answer these questions:

- What's one thing my family did with money that I want to keep doing? (Example: My dad always saved 10 percent of his paycheck, no matter what.)
- What's one thing I'll do differently? (Example: I won't ignore credit card statements like Mom did.)

Jot down your thoughts. And no, this isn't to blame anyone but to spot patterns so you can rewrite them. Awareness is the first step to change.

Give a Little, Gain a Lot

Sharing money feels counterintuitive, but it works. Start small: If you earn $50 babysitting, set aside five to help someone else. Buy a meal for a friend stressing over rent, or donate to a cause you care about, like planting trees or helping stray pets. The goal isn't to fix the world overnight—it's to prove to yourself that money isn't just for you. When you do this from time to time, you rewire your brain to see cash as a way to connect, not just collect (Anders n.d.).

Picture Your Future Self

Retirement sounds like a "someday" problem, but isn't it reassuring and cool to be debt-free and spend winters in a cozy cabin or volunteering abroad when you're sixty-five? How do you get there? Break it into tiny steps. If you save $20 a month starting now, you'll have 12,000 by the time you're fifty (thanks to compound interest, which we will discuss later!). Even if you're saving for a car or college right now, habit-building today means less scrambling tomorrow.

Believe You're Built to Win

No matter your background—to borrow lyrics from *every* nineties boy band—you've got what it takes to succeed. Take it from Maria, a seventeenyear-old who paid cash for her first car by dog-sitting: "I kept messing up my budget at first. But after three months, I stopped overspending at the mall because I knew exactly how much I needed to hit my goal." Start by celebrating tiny wins, like saving $10 a week or negotiating a higher side hustle rate. Belief grows from action—not the other way around.

Emotional Spending

Another important factor in managing money is understanding emotional spending. Have you ever felt bored, stressed, or sad and ended up spending money just to feel better? Maybe you bought an expensive sweatshirt after a rough day or treated yourself to extra snacks even though you weren't hungry. While buying something new feels exciting at first, this feeling quickly fades, leaving you with less money and sometimes regret.

Break this habit by recognizing emotional triggers. Next time you feel like spending impulsively, pause and ask yourself, "Am I buying this because I truly need or want it, or am I just feeling down?" Maybe talk to a friend, listen to music, or do something relaxing instead. Finding healthier ways to cope with your emotions will help your wallet—and your mood—in the long run.

Another trick to cultivating a positive money mindset is focusing on longterm goals instead of short-term wants. Let's say you want to save for a new phone. Each time you're tempted by smaller purchases like fast food or impulse buys, remind yourself of the bigger goal. Is that ten-dollar meal worth it today, or would you rather put it toward your goal? This small habit of thinking ahead helps build patience and discipline.

One great way to shift your thinking is through daily affirmations, positive statements you repeat regularly. Try saying things like: "I'm great at

- managing my money."
- "I make smart financial choices every day."
- "I feel confident and relaxed about money."
- "I have a healthy relationship with money."

Repeating these affirmations each morning sets a positive tone for your day and helps build a confident attitude about your finances.

Mindful Spending

Another helpful habit is mindful spending. This means paying attention and thinking carefully before making a purchase. Mindful spending has four aspects: intentionality, awareness, reflection, and alignment with goals (Calm n.d.). Let's dive deeper into each one of them.

Intentionality means slowing down before you spend. Instead of grabbing that flashy hoodie just because your friend has it or swiping your card mindlessly at the checkout line, take a breath. Ask yourself: "Is this worth trading hours of my time?" For example, if you spent three hours babysitting to earn $30, would you trade that effort for a new video game you'll play once? Being intentional turns spending from a reflex into a choice you control.

Awareness, aside from being the first step to change, is also about understanding why you spend. Maybe you're bored, stressed about exams, or trying to keep up with what you see online (spoiler: 85 percent of teens admit social media influences their purchases) (Walk-Morris 2023). Awareness helps you spot patterns, like realizing you always order takeout when you're procrastinating on homework. Once you see those habits, you can redirect your cash toward what actually fuels your happiness—like saving for spring break with friends instead of blowing cash on temporary distractions.

Reflection is where the magic happens. At the end of each week, take five minutes to review where your money went. Did that forty-dollar sneaker sale leave you with buyer's remorse? Did skipping daily coffee runs help you save up for KPOP tickets? You're not judging yourself—you're learning.

Finally, alignment with your goals ties it all together. You see money as a teammate helping you reach what you care about. If your goal is to buy a used car by graduation, spending fifty a week on fast food nights slows you down. But if your goal is to start a small side hustle—like selling custom sneakers or tutoring— budgeting $20 a week toward supplies or marketing helps you grow without feeling restricted. When your goals are aligned, you avoid random spending while stepping toward the life you're designing.

Mindful spending isn't about being perfect. It's about progress. Start small: Next time you're tempted to buy something, pause and ask, "Does this match who I am—and who I want to be?" So, before clicking "buy," pause and ask yourself:

- "Do I really need this right now?"
- "Will this purchase matter to me tomorrow, next week, or next month?"
- "Is this spending aligned with my goals?"

This simple pause can prevent impulse purchases and help your money go further.

Journaling Exercise

Grab a notebook or use a notes app on your phone to track your financial mindset each week. Write down when you felt stressed or happy about money. Notice what triggered these feelings. Did you spend money impulsively after a tough day at school? Did you resist a tempting buy and feel proud?

Each week, list a few things you're grateful for financially. Maybe you saved extra money from your allowance, avoided buying something unnecessary, or hit a savings goal. Celebrating these small victories helps build a healthier, more positive view of your finances.

Changing your money mindset doesn't happen overnight—but that's okay. With each mindful choice, daily affirmation, and journal entry, you're building confidence and setting yourself up for future financial success. Remember that you control your money; your money doesn't control you.

DO YOU REALLY NEED THAT?

Have you ever walked into your favorite store, spotted something you loved, and immediately wanted to buy it—even though it wasn't on your shopping list? Maybe it was the newest sneakers, a dress you saw on social media, or an expensive console that just dropped. The temptation to buy can be intense. But before you swipe your card or hand over your cash, ask yourself one important question: Do I really need this, or do I just want it?

Knowing the difference between needs and wants can totally change the way you handle money. Here's the simple way to look at it:

- Needs are things you must have to live and stay healthy. Think of food, water, a safe place to live, electricity, clothing, and basic medical care. These are the expenses you absolutely can't skip.
- Wants are items or experiences that make your life more enjoyable but aren't necessary. Examples include streaming subscriptions, new accessories, fast food, concert tickets, and even the latest smartphone model.

For example, your friend Olivia might insist she "needs" the newest iPhone. But does she really? Her current phone works fine —it texts, calls, and streams just as well as before. She can even play a high-graphics game on it. What Olivia truly has is a "want," and while it's completely fine to want nice things, knowing when to buy them and when to hold back is key to avoiding money problems later.

One easy way to handle your money smartly is using the 50/30/20 rule. Here's how it works:

- Fifty percent of your money goes toward your needs (like food, transportation, phone bills, or other necessary expenses).

- Thirty percent is for your wants (clothes, entertainment, hanging out with friends).
- Twenty percent goes into your savings (for emergencies, college, or big future goals).

Let's say you earned $100 this month. Following this rule, you would put fifty aside to cover necessary costs, spend thirty on something fun like going to the movies or grabbing food with your friends, and then save the remaining twenty for something bigger down the road.

Another super-useful strategy is creating a wish list for things you really want. Every time you see something you'd love to have, write it down instead of immediately buying it. This gives you a cooling-off period, which helps you think clearly about whether you truly want the item or just felt excited at the moment. After waiting a few days or weeks, many would find that they don't care about those items as much anymore—saving themselves money and buyer's remorse.

Speaking of regret, let's talk about impulsive buying—those quick, unplanned purchases that seem exciting at first but often lead to disappointment later. Dylan spends his entire paycheck impulsively buying shoes he saw on TikTok. The excitement might feel great initially, but now Dylan has no money left for things like gas, lunch at school, or even a simple weekend hangout. He might even need to borrow money or use a credit card, putting himself in debt just for a pair of sneakers!

To avoid these situations, try using the twenty-four-hour rule. The next time you're tempted by a sudden purchase, wait a whole day before buying. Chances are, after sleeping on it, you'll either forget about the item or realize it's not as urgent or exciting as it initially seemed.

Another fantastic way to manage your money better is keeping a spending tracker. You can do this on your phone, using notes or an app that shows exactly where your cash goes each week. Seeing it visually can help you quickly identify patterns. Maybe you'll be shocked to see how much you're spending on snacks or gaming, or you'll be surprised at how much you can save by skipping your daily dose of iced coffee. Recognizing these habits makes it easier to redirect money toward more important or rewarding goals.

At the bottom line, prioritizing needs over wants doesn't mean you can't have fun or buy nice things. It's as simple as making thoughtful decisions that line up with your goals. The feeling of treating yourself after saving up is often much more satisfying than quick, impulse-driven buys. Besides, spending wisely gives

you freedom and the power to say yes to things you truly care about.

MONEY SMARTS CHALLENGE: REALITY CHECK

Grab a notebook or open a note-taking app, and let's put your new money skills into practice. This quick challenge will show you exactly how your spending aligns with your goals and values.

- Step 1: Reality Check Log
  - For one whole week, write down every single purchase you make—no exceptions. Whether it's snacks, music downloads, clothes, or online purchases, note it down along with the amount. At the end of the week, sort your expenses into two columns: needs and wants.
- Step 2: Reflection Time
  - Now answer these questions honestly: Did you
    - spend more on wants or needs? Which purchases
    - felt really worth it, and which made you feel regretful afterward?
    - Could you have saved or redirected some money to a bigger goal?
- Step 3: Action Plan
  - Based on what you discovered, write down one thing you'll do differently next week, like packing snacks from home, cutting back on impulse purchases, or setting a small weekly savings goal.

Repeat this Reality Check Log monthly, and soon you'll become a pro at aligning your spending with what's important to you!

Great job! Now that you've seen firsthand how your spending choices impact your life, you're ready to start building a budget that helps you save smarter, reach your goals faster, and manage your money with confidence. In the next chapter, you'll learn easy strategies for budgeting.

2

BUDGETING BASICS: KNOWING WHERE YOUR MONEY IS GOING

Have you ever started planning an awesome weekend with friends—a pizza night or hitting the mall—only to realize your wallet can't keep up with your plans? It's a frustrating feeling, especially when you know you're missing out. But what if there was a way to enjoy all the things you love without feeling broke afterward?

Good news: Budgeting is another approach to help you have even more fun without stress. In a way, a budget will make your money work smarter, not harder. In this chapter, you'll learn how to enjoy the things you care about most without the guilt or worry of running low on cash.

YOUR FIRST BUDGET

If the idea of making a budget sounds boring or complicated, you're not alone. In fact, about 30 percent of Gen Z don't follow a monthly budget (Butts 2024). One reason is that most teens assume budgeting means giving up fun or being strict about every penny (I used to think this way, too!). But in reality, creating a budget actually gives you more control and freedom. It's like having a GPS for your money—guiding you exactly where you want it to go and helping you reach your goals faster.

So, how do you start? NerdWallet breaks it down into easy steps:

- **Step One: Know What You're Working With**
    - Start by figuring out your monthly take-home pay—the cash that actually lands in your bank account after taxes. If you have a steady job, this is your net income (what's left after taxes, insurance, or retirement savings are deducted). Pro tip: If you're freelancing or doing gig work, subtract taxes and work costs (like gas or supplies) from your earnings to see your real profit.
- **Step Two: Pick a Method That Fits**
    - Budgeting isn't one-size-fits-all. Choose a system that matches your habits, such as the envelope system, where you divide cash into labeled envelopes for different categories like "food" or "fun." The 50/30/20 rule we previously talked about is another practical budgeting method, too. Whatever it is you choose, your budget should cover essentials (like phone bills), fun stuff (like streaming services), and savings.
- **Step Three: Keep Tabs on Where Your Cash Goes** Track your
    - spending for a month using a notebook, spreadsheet, or free app. Look for patterns: Are you overspending on takeout? Could you cut back on subscriptions you barely use? Redirect any extra cash toward goals like paying off a phone plan or boosting your emergency fund.
- **Step Four: Make Saving Effortless**
    - Set up automatic transfers to savings or investments right after payday. If your income's unpredictable (like from babysitting or selling art), schedule manual transfers whenever you get paid.
- **Step Five: Tweak as You Go**
    - Life changes, and so should your budget. Every few months, ask:
        - Are my goals the same? (e.g., saving for a car vs. college textbooks) Is my current method stressing me out?
        - Do I need to adjust for new expenses (like a gym membership)?
        - It's okay to switch systems—the goal is to find what keeps you
    - motivated (Schwahn 2025)!

Budget Smarter with Tech

The good news is that budgeting is easier than ever thanks to apps you can download right to your phone. Apps like Acorns, Goodbudget, FamZoo, GoHenry, Greenlight, and You Need a Budget (YNAB) track your spending automatically, categorize expenses, and show you exactly where your money goes (Arizona Central Credit Union 2023). These apps also let you set spending limits and send helpful reminders when you're close to overspending. It's like having a personal assistant who keeps an eye on your cash for you!

For example, someone I know always struggled to save money. Let's call him Jordan. When he started using GoHenry, instead of feeling surprised every time his money ran out, he got notifications when he spent too much on video games or snacks. These gentle nudges helped Jordan change his spending habits—and he even managed to save enough for a skateboard he'd wanted for months!

COMMON MISTAKES (AND HOW TO AVOID THEM)

Budgeting isn't always easy, especially in the beginning. Here are some common slip-ups teens often make—and easy ways to avoid them.

Mistake One: Skipping Emergency Savings

Let's face it—unexpected expenses will happen: a flat tire, a sudden phone repair, or an unexpected medical emergency, you name it. Nearly half of Americans can't cover a $1,000 emergency without debt (Lee 2025). Start small: Treat savings like a monthly bill, even if it's just $20. Automate transfers to a separate account (like a high-yield savings option, which we will discuss later) or tuck away cash from side gigs. The goal isn't to save six months' worth of expenses overnight—it's to build a safety net so life's surprises don't derail your progress.

Mistake Two: Overestimating Your Spending Cash

We've all been there: You think you have $150 left for the month, only to realize bills ate up half of it. This happens most when you forget taxes, rely on pre-tax income numbers, or face irregular paychecks. To fix it, base your budget on your lowest income month (if your job isn't steady) and track every dollar for thirty days. Apps or even a notes page on your phone can help spot patterns, like overspending on delivery apps.

Mistake Three: Ignoring Fun Money Entirely

Cutting out all fun to "save more" sounds logical, but it's a fast track to burnout. Like in dieting, if you ban pizza forever, you'll eventually binge. Instead, allocate guilt-free cash for things you enjoy—like hobbies and interests (writing, singing, dancing, or playing a sport). This keeps you motivated and stops spur-of-themoment splurges. I know someone who set aside $15 weekly for thrift store shopping, which helped her stick to her bigger goal of saving for a car.

Mistake Four: Treating Your Budget Like a One-Time Project

Life changes—fast. Maybe your rent just jumped, you're juggling college apps, or gas prices doubled. A budget that worked six months ago might not fit now. Revisit it every few months to ask: Does this still match my goals? If you're consistently overspending in one area (like groceries), adjust instead of beating yourself up. Flexibility is important. For example, after getting a part-time job, one teen shifted her budget to save 10 percent of each paycheck for a laptop instead of sticking to her old "allowance-only" plan.

LIVING BIG ON A SMALL BUDGET

You don't need a huge bank account to have an awesome time. If you're creative, careful, and a little bit clever, you can do a lot with just a little. Let's say you're hosting a themed potluck night with friends. Everyone brings a dish, maybe based on a country or a color, and suddenly, you've got an entire evening of fun, food, and laughs—for next to nothing. It's way cheaper than going out to eat, and honestly, it's usually a lot more memorable. Let's change the common thought that fun comes with a high price tag because it doesn't have to be.

Fun doesn't have to come with a high price tag. There are tons of ways to enjoy life, hang out with friends, and treat yourself without draining your account.

Hidden Perks: Use the Discounts You Already Have

Being a student has its perks. A lot of places offer student discounts—you just have to know where to look. Flash your student ID at the movie theater, and you might score a cheaper ticket. Same with public transportation, local attractions, and even software or tech subscriptions. Below are some retailers offering student discounts:

- **Discounts on Electronics**
    - Students can save significantly on tech with verified discounts. Apple offers gift cards of up to $150 and 20 percent off AppleCare+ with purchases of MacBook or iPad devices, along with 3 percent cash back for Apple Card holders. Best Buy's Back to School Student Hub often features exclusive deals for students. HP provides up to 40 percent off through its Education Store, while Lenovo adds an extra 5 percent discount for students verified via ID.me. Logitech offers up to 30 percent off for UNiDAYS members, and Microsoft extends 10 percent off on select products. Samsung rounds out the list with up to 30 percent off for students enrolled in its Education Offers Program.
- **Discounts at Restaurants**
    - While many restaurants keep student discounts unadvertised, some chains openly cater to budgets. Arby's, Buffalo Wild

Wings, and Burger King offer up to 10 percent off at participating locations, while Chick-fil-A provides a free small drink with any purchase. DoorDash reduces its DashPass subscription to $4.99 per month for students, and Dunkin' offers 10 percent off at select stores.

- **Discounts on Software**
    - Essential software subscriptions become more affordable with student deals. Adobe Creative Cloud drops to $19.99 per month for the first year, and Amazon Prime Student is free for six months before charging half price ($7.49 per month). Evernote Professional is discounted by 40 percent annually, while Microsoft Office 365 Personal costs $2.99 per month with 1TB of cloud storage. Slack Pro plans are 85 percent off for classroom use; Spotify bundles Premium and Hulu (with ads) for $5.99 per month; and YouTube Premium's student plan is $7.99 per month.
- **Discounts on Clothing**
    - Fashion brands cater to student budgets with verified discounts. Adidas, Aeropostale, and J.Crew offer 15 percent off; American Eagle and Calvin Klein provide up to 20 percent off select items. H&M and Nike extend 10 percent off, and Meshki matches with 15 percent off. For additional brands, UNiDAYS lists hundreds of student-exclusive deals (Rodriguez et al., 2025).

These discounts can cut your spending way down. If you're not sure, just ask! "Do you offer a student discount?" is a great question that could save you cash often.

Thrift Like a Pro

Luxury doesn't always mean brand new or expensive. Thrift stores are goldmines. You can score stylish clothes, cool accessories, and even vintage pieces for a fraction of regular prices. It's like going on a treasure hunt—sometimes, you find something totally unique that no one else will have. Below are some tips from The Good Trade to make the most out of your thrift shopping:

- **Plan Ahead**
    - Thrift shopping without a plan is like grocery shopping hungry—you'll end up with items you don't need. Before heading out, jot down gaps in your wardrobe (e.g., a neutral blazer or vintage jeans) and save inspiration photos to your phone. This keeps you focused and helps store staff assist you better.
- **Sell Before You Shop**
    - Clear closet space and fund new finds by selling clothes you no longer wear. Many thrift stores offer consignment options where you can trade items for store credit or cash. Online platforms like Poshmark or Depop work too —just snap pics of your pieces and let buyers come to you.
- **Dress Strategically**
    - Wear form-fitting layers (like a tank top and leggings) to try clothes over your outfit if fitting rooms are unavailable. Comfortable shoes and a crossbody bag are essential for marathon browsing sessions. Shopping online? Keep a tape measure handy and compare your stats to brand size charts.
- **Stick to Cash**
    - Leave cards at home and bring only the cash you're willing to spend. This forces you to prioritize pieces that truly fit your style and needs. Admire quirky items, but ask: Will I wear this more than once? If not, snap a photo and move on.
- **Scan, Don't Stare**
    - Save time by training your eye to spot colors, textures, or patterns that match your aesthetic. Skim racks quickly—stop only for pieces that

jump out. Online? Use filters for size, color, or material to narrow options fast.

- **Prioritize Fabric Quality**
  - Natural fibers like cotton and wool age gracefully but may need gentle care. Synthetics like polyester are durable but less eco-friendly. Always check garment tags (or use your phone's flashlight to inspect seams and hems for wear).
- **Think Outside the Aisle**
  - Men's sections hide oversized sweaters and vintage jackets, while kids' racks offer cropped tees at lower prices. Browse lingerie for slip dresses or corsets, and don't skip accessories—belts and scarves can transform basics.
- **Inspect, Inspect, Inspect**
  - Check for stains, holes, or loose buttons under bright light. Test zippers and seams, and flip items inside out to spot hidden flaws. Online shoppers: Review photos closely and message sellers about imperfections before buying.
- **Tailor Your Treasures**
  - A too-long dress or boxy blazer can become a staple with simple alterations. Learn basic sewing for hems or take pieces to a tailor for adjustments—just ensure the cost doesn't outweigh the item's value.
- **Befriend Store Staff**
  - Regulars get the scoop on restock days and first dibs on new arrivals. Chat with employees—they'll often share tips or hold items for you. Plus, they're great at honest feedback ("Does this jacket scream 'you'?") (The Good Trade 2024).

Smart Travel = Affordable Adventures

Are you dreaming of a trip but don't want to go broke? Here are three tips for planning it smart.

- **Master Flight Hacks**
    - Finding affordable flights starts with the right tools. Use platforms like Google Flights (flexible date grids) or Skyscanner (price alerts and "Everywhere" search) to compare options. Sign up for email alerts from sites like Scott's Cheap Flights or Secret Flying to snag error fares or flash sales. Pro tip: Midweek flights (Tuesdays/Wednesdays) often cost less—adjust your dates if possible.
- **Turn Layovers into Mini-Trips**
    - Long layovers don't have to mean airport boredom. Many airlines (like Icelandair or TAP Portugal) offer free stopover programs, letting you explore a city for days en route to your final destination. Example: Fly from New York to Paris via Reykjavik and spend fortyeight hours soaking in Iceland's hot springs. Check airline policies beforehand—some even throw in discounted hotels or tours.
- **Rethink Where You Sleep**
    - Accommodation eats budgets fast, but alternatives exist:
        - **Night Travel:** Take overnight buses/trains between cities to save on a hotel.
        - **Couchsurfing:** Crash with locals for free (safety first—read reviews and verify profiles).
        - **House Sitting:** Trade pet care or plant watering for free stays.
        - **Volunteer Stays:** There are platforms that connect travelers with hosts needing help (e.g., hostel work, farming) in exchange for lodging, meals, or tours. These gigs let you stay longer, dive into local culture, and stretch your budget (Helen 2023).

With a little planning, that weekend getaway isn't out of reach—it's totally possible.

Compare, Ask, and Save

Want to stretch your dollars even further? Start comparing prices before you buy. There are apps that let you scan barcodes or search items and show you where to get the best deal. It's an easy way to stop overpaying, especially for big purchases. This Shopifycurated list is my go-to reference for these apps:

- Google Shopping
- Shopzilla
- Become
- Bizrate
- Camelcamelcamel
- ShopMania
- BuyVia
- ShopSavvy
- Yahoo! Shopping
- Pricepirates
- Twenga
- Price.com (Hayes 2025)

And don't be afraid to ask for a better price—especially at local shops or markets. Polite negotiating isn't rude; it's smart! Practice being confident and respectful, and you might be surprised by how often people say yes.

Zero-Based Budgeting: Give Every Dollar a Job

One simple but powerful method to manage your money is something called zero-based budgeting. It just means that when you plan your budget, your total income minus all your expenses (including savings) should equal zero. Every dollar you earn gets assigned a role—no leftovers, no random spending.

Here's the formula:

Money you earn - Money you plan to spend/save = $0

Even if you're saving, that money has a job—it's just sitting in a savings account instead of being spent. This system helps you avoid random "Where did my money go?" moments. It keeps your spending purposeful and your savings growing.

Fidelity Smart Money proposes a simple four-step guide (n.d.):

- **Step One: Know Your Monthly Income**
    - First, figure out how much money you get each month. That includes paychecks, side jobs, or anything else that brings in cash.

      If your income changes month to month, look at your lowestearning month from the past year and use that as your starting point. That way, you're not spending money you might not have.
- **Step Two: Write Down What You'll Spend and Save**
    - Next, make a list of what you need to pay for. This includes stuff like:
        - Rent or housing
        - Food
        - Transportation
        - Bills
        - School supplies
        - Debt (if you have any)
    - Fun stuff (like going out, clothes, or streaming) Also include savings—like money you're putting away for the future or emergencies.

      Set an amount for each category based on what you think you'll spend.
- **Step Three: Subtract It All from Your Income**
    - Take your total income and subtract everything on your list. You want the final number to be zero. That means every dollar has a job. If the

number is negative, you're spending too much. Cut back on things you don't need. If the number is positive, decide where that extra money should go—like savings or something fun you've been planning.

- **Step Four: Check In at the End of the Month**
  - Your budget is a plan—but plans can change. At the end of the month, compare what you spent to what you planned. Did anything surprise you? Did you overspend? If something keeps popping up, add it to next month's budget. If you're going over in certain areas, try using cash only for those—when the money's gone, you're done spending.

If your income changes from month to month, just work with an average. And don't worry—you can update your budget anytime if something unexpected comes up.

Ditch the Sneaky Fees

Those "only $10 a month" subscriptions add up fast. If you've got more than one streaming service, music app, or other monthly subscription, go through them and see what you actually use. You might be paying for Spotify and Apple Music when you only really use one. Or maybe you forgot you subscribed to something during a free trial. Cancel the stuff you don't use—those dollars can be put to way better use elsewhere.

Plan Your Meals (Your Wallet Will Thank You)

Buying lunch or snacks on the go adds up fast. Instead, plan your meals ahead of time. Make a grocery list, pick meals that share ingredients, and only buy what you'll actually use. You'll waste less food, eat better, and spend way less.

MyPlate.gov gives us some tips to get started with meal planning:

Check What You Already Have: Look through your fridge, freezer, and pantry. You might already have ingredients you can use, which means fewer things to buy.

Write Down Your Weekly Menu: Decide what you want to eat for breakfast, lunch, dinner, and snacks each day.

Write it all down so you're not guessing last minute. **Pick a Few New Recipes:** Want to try something different? Find easy, low-cost meals based on what you already have at home. Stick with affordable meals your family likes.

Keep Your Schedule in Mind: Busy days call for quick meals. Save the longer recipes for weekends or when someone can help you cook.

Plan to Have Leftovers: Make extra food when you cook. Leftovers make a great backup when you're short on time or don't feel like cooking again.

Make a Shopping List: Before you head to the store, list everything you'll need. Group items by section—like produce, dairy, frozen—to make shopping faster. **Add Items as You Run Out:** Keep a running list on your fridge or phone. Add things the moment you run out so you don't forget later. You can even use apps to share lists with others in your home.

Mix It Up with Different Types of Food: Get a variety— fresh, frozen, and canned foods all work. Eat fresh stuff first so it doesn't spoil, and keep pantry or freezer items around for later in the week (MyPlate.gov n.d.).

You don't have to become a chef overnight—just aim to plan a few meals in advance each week. You'll probably find you're eating healthier without even trying.

Pay Yourself First

When your paycheck or allowance comes in, it can be tempting to spend first and think about saving later. Try flipping that. The minute you get paid, put a portion—whatever you can afford— into your savings. Even $5 adds up over time. NerdWallet lays out four simple steps to paying yourself first:

- **Step One: Look at Your Spending Habits**
    - Before you start saving, get a good idea of how you usually spend your money. Pull up your bank and credit card statements and review the past month or two. Don't aim too high right away—start small. You can always increase your savings later. It's better to save a little consistently than to go big and end up short on cash.
- **Step Two: Choose How Much to Save**
    - Use the 50/30/20 rule to guide you. If you earn $200 a month, that means $40 goes to saving and paying off debt. Try to keep savings a priority.
- **Step Three: Set Your Savings Goals**
    - Decide what you're saving for. Some common goals include:
        - Building an emergency fund
        - Saving for college
        - Buying a new phone or laptop
        - Going on a trip
    - Using the same example above, you'd try to save around $40. You might decide to put twenty-five toward your emergency fund and fifteen toward a fun goal. Save that money first—before spending on anything else.
- **Step Four: Tweak Your Plan as You Go**
    - If you're having trouble covering everything, don't panic. It's okay to make changes. You might:

Focus on one savings goal at a time.

Cut back on extra spending.

- Look for ways to earn a little more on the side. The point is to keep paying yourself first, even if the amount changes now and then (Schwahn 2024-b).

Turn Money into Time: Is It Worth Your Hours?

Money isn't just numbers in your bank account—it represents time, effort, and energy. One way to think more carefully about spending is to connect every dollar to how long it takes to earn it.

For example, let's say someone earns $15 an hour. A purchase that costs $60 would take four hours of work to pay for. That's half a day of standing on your feet, dealing with customers, or completing tasks. So before spending, it's helpful to ask: Is this item really worth four hours of effort? This way of thinking turns money into something more personal. Instead of just seeing a price tag, you start seeing the real cost in time. And when time is something you don't get back, every dollar starts to matter more.

Doing so can make it easier to skip impulse buys and focus on saving for things that are actually meaningful—like a new phone, future plans, or simply peace of mind. When money is treated with respect, it can help build the kind of life that feels good—not just in the moment but later, too.

By building smart habits now—like comparing prices, paying yourself first, or seeing cash beyond its monetary worth—you're setting yourself up for a strong financial future. Living well on a budget is about making choices that help you get the most out of your money and your life.

MONEY SMARTS CHALLENGE: ARE YOU REALLY IN CONTROL OF YOUR CASH?

Now that you've learned how to build a budget that actually works, it's time to check in with yourself by asking these questions:

- Do I know exactly how much money I get each month— and where it all goes?
- Which expenses are totally necessary, and which ones could I cut back without much regret?
- Is there a spending habit that's costing me more than it's worth?
- When I make a purchase, am I thinking ahead or just reacting in the moment?
- Have I ever made a budget and actually stuck to it—even for one week?
- How would I feel if I needed to cover a surprise expense tomorrow?
- What's one money-related habit I want to change starting now?

There's no grade here—just honesty. These questions aren't about guilt or perfection. They're about getting real with yourself and your money. The more aware you are of your habits, the easier it becomes to make changes that actually stick.

Once you've built a solid budget, you start to see where your money is really going—and that's when saving gets real. A budget shows you what's possible, but saving turns those possibilities into progress. Whether you're dreaming of a new phone, planning for college, or just want to stop feeling broke all the time, saving gives you the freedom to get there without the stress. Shall we?

3

SAVE IT LIKE YOU MEAN IT

One second, your phone is fine, and the next, it's cracked and unusable. Or maybe your bike breaks down the day before school starts. When stuff like that happens—and it will— having some money set aside makes all the difference. That's what a backup plan is for, and to build one, you need to save.

HOW TO BUILD A BACKUP PLAN THAT ACTUALLY WORKS

Saving doesn't have to be stressful or only for adults with full-time jobs. Anyone can start building a safety net, no matter how small their income. Even $50 or $100 in savings can be enough to cover basic emergencies. That small backup fund can save you from needing to borrow money or miss out on something important. Start with one simple goal: Set aside enough to cover at least one surprise expense. Maybe it's fixing a broken screen, replacing a lost charger, or paying for an unexpected school cost. When you have savings, these situations don't feel like a disaster—they're just something you deal with.

The first step is deciding what you're saving for. It helps to set specific goals instead of a vague idea like "saving more." For example, maybe you want to save $200 in four months. That's $50 a month. When you break it into smaller pieces, it feels less overwhelming and way more doable. You might not hit every goal perfectly every month, and that's okay. Some weeks, you might be able to save more, and others, you might fall a little short. What matters is staying consistent. Saving a little over time builds momentum. The habit itself is more important than the exact amount.

There are easy ways to build this habit into your daily life. You can toss your spare change into a jar. Round up your purchases and save the difference. Every time you skip a small purchase—like that second iced coffee— transfer the money to your savings. You're not depriving yourself; you're being and having something to show for it. To stay motivated, try tracking your progress visually. Seeing the numbers grow, even slowly, gives you a boost. It's proof that your effort is working.

Another useful trick is to separate your savings from your spending money. Keep it in a different bank account or digital wallet. If it's not mixed in with your regular cash, you're less likely to touch it impulsively. Some teens even rename their savings accounts things like "Emergency Fund Only" or "Do Not Touch," just as a little reminder.

Saving gets easier once it becomes part of your routine. After a while, you'll start planning for it the same way you plan for your monthly phone bill or streaming service. The more you treat saving like a priority, the more natural it feels. You may also notice a shift in how you think about money because the feeling of always playing catch-up will slowly fade. That confidence can change how you handle everyday decisions. You'll feel more prepared, less stressed, and more focused on what really matters!

Here are some savings challenges to try:

- **The $5 Challenge**
    - Every time you get a $5 bill, save it. No spending—just stash it in a jar, envelope, or your savings app. It adds up fast without feeling like a big deal.
- **The No-Spend Weekend**
    - Pick one weekend a month to spend nothing. No shopping, no apps, no fast food. Find free things to do and transfer what you would've spent into savings.

- **Save Your Coins Challenge**
  - At the end of each day, drop your loose change (or leftover small bills) into a jar. When it's full, count it up and move it to savings, or use it toward something you've been planning for.
- **A Dollar-a-Day Challenge**
  - Save $1 a day for a full month. That's $30 saved without stress. Once that's easy, bump it up to $2 or more. It's all about building the habit.
- **Spend-Match Challenge**
  - Anytime you spend money on something fun—like clothes, fast food, or games—match that amount by saving the same. It makes you think twice and grows your savings faster.
- **Digital Detox Challenge**
  - Take a one-day break from online shopping, food delivery apps, and anything that makes you want to spend money with a tap. At the end of the day, move $10 into savings as a reward for staying offline. Try this once a week and watch your money pile up.

Saving is a choice you make for your future self. It doesn't require perfection. It just takes a little consistency, a plan that makes sense for you, and the belief that you're worth preparing for.

SET IT AND FORGET IT: LET YOUR SAVINGS GROW ON AUTOPILOT

What if saving money didn't require daily effort or decisionmaking? That's the power of automation. Once set up, automatic savings move money into your account without you having to do anything else. It's one of the easiest and most effective ways to stay on track financially, especially when life gets busy.

Start by thinking about how much you can realistically save from each paycheck. It doesn't have to be a lot. Even $5 or $10 every week adds up as long as they're automatic. Once the transfer is set to repeat, you won't even notice the money leaving your account— but you will definitely notice your savings growing.

If you're earning money from a part-time job or getting a regular allowance, ask about direct deposit. Many banks let you split your deposit between a checking and savings account. You can choose to send a percentage—say, 10 or 20 percent—directly into savings before the rest hits your spending account. This way, saving becomes your default instead of something you try to squeeze in later.

You can also schedule recurring transfers on your own. Most banking apps or websites make it easy to set up a weekly or monthly transfer. Choose an amount, pick the date, and let the app handle the rest. If payday is every Friday, set the transfer for Saturday morning. The money will move before you have a chance to spend it on things you might regret.

To make your savings go even further, consider using a high-yield savings account. These accounts usually offer better interest rates (often ten to twenty times higher) than regular savings accounts. That means your money grows faster, even when you're not adding to it. Look for one with no monthly fees and easy access when needed—but not too easy, so you're not tempted to dip into it just because it's there.

If you want to take it a step further, there are apps designed to help automate saving in ways that don't feel like a chore. Here's a list by US News:

- Acorns
- Oportun
- Chime
- Albert
- Rocket Money (Egan 2025)

Some of these apps round up your purchases and save the spare change for you. For example, if you spend $3.45 on a coffee, it rounds up to $4.00 and moves the extra $0.55 into your savings. You don't miss the change, but it quietly adds up in the background. Other apps monitor your spending patterns and transfer small amounts into savings based on what they think you can afford. It's low effort, low pressure, and surprisingly effective.

Automated savings also come with mental benefits. Knowing that money is being set aside regularly—without needing to think about it—takes a lot of the pressure off. It helps reduce stress around money decisions and creates a strong sense of stability (Tippla 2024). You don't have to constantly worry about whether you remembered to save or if you'll have enough set aside for emergencies.

Automation also helps avoid something called decision fatigue. That's what happens when you're tired of making so many small choices throughout the day. Saving money can feel like one more task on an already long list. But when you automate it, you remove that decision entirely (Truist n.d.). It becomes part of your routine —like brushing your teeth or packing your backpack.

MONEY SMARTS CHALLENGE: BUDGET AND SAVE LIKE A BOSS

Now that you've seen how easy it can be to "set it and forget it," let's put your new budgeting and saving skills into action. This challenge is all about testing what you've learned—and finding out just how much progress you can make when you stick to a plan.

Step One: Build Your Budget

Start by writing down how much money you receive in a typical month. This could be from a job, allowance, or side hustle like babysitting or tutoring. Then, list your monthly expenses. Be honest about what you usually spend. Include things like:

- Subscriptions or memberships
- Eating out or ordering in
- School supplies or transportation Entertainment, clothes, or apps
-

Next, divide your spending into two categories: needs and wants. Use what you learned earlier to label them clearly.

Finally, use the 50/30/20 guideline as a starting point. Adjust the numbers if necessary. The goal is to create a plan that works for you. ***Step Two: Automate Your Savings***

If you haven't already, set up an automatic transfer—weekly, biweekly, or monthly. It can be any amount that fits your budget. Not ready to use a bank? Use a labeled envelope, jar, or digital wallet to put aside money right when you get it. What matters most is building the habit.

Step Three: Track & Reflect

At the end of the month, answer these questions in your journal or phone notes:

- Did your budget help you stay on track?
- Were there any surprises in your spending?
- How did it feel to save automatically?
- What would you change for next month?

Saving gives you control over your money—but that's just the beginning. Next up, we'll talk about something that can either open doors or cause major setbacks if you're not careful: credit. In the next chapter, you'll learn what it really means, why it matters, and how to build it the smart way—starting now.

4

UNDERSTANDING AND BUILDING CREDIT

A recent survey by BadCredit.org found that nearly one-third of Americans—31 percent—don't know their credit score (Spector 2023). That's a huge deal, especially when you realize how much power that one number holds. Your credit score can affect everything from getting a phone plan to renting an apartment, taking out a loan, or even landing certain jobs.

If you've never heard much about credit, it's understandable. Most schools don't teach it, and adults don't always talk about it. But learning how credit works—and how to build it the smart way— can set you up for serious advantages down the line. That's what we'll do in this chapter: break down what credit is, why you need to know about it, how to build it from scratch, and what to watch out for so you don't end up with regrets later.

WHAT IS A CREDIT SCORE AND WHY YOU SHOULD CARE

You've probably heard adults talk about credit scores and how they can affect everything from getting a car to renting an apartment. It might sound like something far off in the future, but understanding credit now can help you avoid a lot of stress later.

So, what is a credit score, and why is it important?

Think of your credit score as a financial reputation—one that tells lenders, landlords, and even some employers how responsible you are with money.

It's a three-digit number, usually between 300 and 850, and it's based on how well you've managed borrowed money. The higher the number, the better.

If you're just getting started with credit, your score might not even exist yet. That's okay. What matters is learning how credit works so you can build a strong score when the time comes.

What Goes into a Credit Score?

Credit scores are calculated using information from your credit report. This report is a detailed history of how you've handled loans, credit cards, and any other form of borrowing. According to Investopedia (2024), here are the key parts that make up a typical score:

Payment History (35 percent): This is the biggest chunk. It shows whether you've paid your bills on time. One or two late payments might not seem like a big deal, but they can bring your score down quickly.

Credit Utilization (30 percent): This measures how much of your available credit you're using. If your credit card limit is $1,000 and you've spent $700, your utilization is 70 percent—and that's high. Most experts recommend keeping it below 30 percent.

Length of Credit History (15 percent): The longer you've had credit, the better—if you've handled it well. This is one reason people suggest starting small, like with a student card or a shared account, as soon as it makes sense.

Credit Mix (10 percent): Lenders like to see that you can handle different types of credit—like credit cards, student loans, or car loans. You don't need to open new accounts just to improve your mix, but it's something that adds up over time.

New Credit Inquiries (10 percent): Every time you apply for a credit card or loan, it's recorded as an inquiry. Too many in a short time can hurt your score, so only apply when necessary.

So, why do you need to know? Your credit score influences more than you might expect. A strong score can help you with various adulting needs you might encounter later on, such as qualifying for loans, getting approved for an apartment, scoring better interest rates, and avoiding larger deposits for things like smartphones or utilities. On the other hand, a low score can make borrowing more expensive—or block you from certain opportunities altogether.

How to Keep Track of Your Credit

You can check your credit score for free using reputable apps or services. Many banks even offer credit score tracking as part of your online account. These tools also break down what's helping or hurting your score and offer tips for improvement.

In addition to checking your score, you should also review your credit report at least once a year. This helps you catch any errors or suspicious activity early. You're entitled to a free report annually from each of the three major credit bureaus: Experian, TransUnion, and Equifax.

Habits That Help You Build a Strong Score

Even if you're not applying for anything now, the habits you build early on—like paying bills on time and keeping your spending in check—will help when you do need credit later. Below are more ways to begin:

Use a Secured Credit Card: This type of card requires a deposit upfront, and that amount becomes your credit limit. It's a low-risk way to start building credit. As long as you pay on time, your credit history grows.

Try a Credit-Builder Loan: Offered by many banks and credit unions, these small loans are designed to help you build credit. You make monthly payments, and once it's paid off, you get access to the money. Every on-time payment helps boost your credit.

Become an Authorized User: Ask a parent or guardian if you can be added to their credit card as an authorized user. Even if you don't use the card, their good payment history can help improve your score.

Make Student Loan Payments: If you have student loans, each on-time payment counts toward your credit history. Some students take out small loans just to build credit, even if they don't need to.

Use a Gas Card: Gas credit cards are another beginnerfriendly option. They often come with small discounts and are easier to qualify for. Just remember to pay your balance off each month.

Watch Your Credit Report: Using a free credit monitoring tool helps you track what's helping or hurting your score. You'll also get alerts if something suspicious happens, which can help you catch fraud early.

Open a Joint Account: You can apply for a loan or credit card with a parent or guardian as a co-signer. This helps you get approved and start building credit with their support.

Get a Student Credit Card: Some credit cards are made just for students and are easier to qualify for. They're a great way to learn how credit works and build up your score at the same time.

Build Good Habits Early: Pay all your bills on time, spend only what you can afford to repay, and try to pay more than the minimum when you can. These habits make a big difference over time.

Report Your Rent: Once you're living on your own, paying rent becomes one of your biggest monthly bills. Services are available that can report those payments to the credit bureaus, helping you build credit just by paying rent on time.

Pay Utility and Phone Bills Promptly: On-time payments for things like your phone or internet bill can help your score—while late payments can hurt it and lead to fees. It's a simple but powerful habit.

Use Educational Tools: Take advantage of credit-building tools made for students. Some services and apps are designed to teach you how credit works while helping you build your score. For example, EVERFI offers free courses just for students (Snellgrove n.d.).

Learning about credit might seem like a lot, but it's actually one of the most empowering things you can do. Your credit score has a real impact on your future, from getting your first apartment to buying a car or even starting a business. Besides, you can build it! You just have to stay informed and build smart habits early.

Now that you know how credit works, it's time to look at how borrowing money really functions—and what you need to understand before taking on any kind of debt.

YOUR FIRST CREDIT CARD: BUILDING CREDIT WITHOUT THE STRESS

Getting your first credit card can feel like a big step—and it is. It marks the beginning of financial independence and shows that someone (a bank or credit company) trusts you enough to lend you money. But with that trust comes responsibility. A credit card isn't free money. It's a tool—and the way you use it can help or hurt your financial future.

Not all credit cards are the same, and picking one that fits your needs can make things easier down the line. American Express shares factors to pay attention to when choosing the best credit card:

Know Your Financial Situation: Before looking at cards, understand your own money habits. Things like your credit score, how much you earn, and how you spend can affect which cards you qualify for. Some cards are meant for building credit, while others offer rewards—usually for people with higher credit scores.

Think About Why You Want a Credit Card: Are you trying to build credit? Earn rewards for travel? Save on interest by moving over a balance from another card? Your reason helps narrow down the best type of card for your needs.

Check Out the Rewards: Some cards give you cash back, and others give you points or miles. Some reward you more in certain spending areas like gas or groceries. Think about where you spend the most—and choose a card that rewards you for it.

Don't Ignore Annual Fees: Some cards charge a yearly fee. Cards with higher fees usually offer better rewards or perks, like airport lounge access. But if you don't use those perks, that fee might not be worth it. Look for a no-fee card if you're just starting out or won't use premium benefits.

Pay Attention to Interest Rates: This is how much you'll owe if you don't pay your balance in full each month. If you plan to carry a balance, look for a card with the lowest interest rate possible—or one with an intro offer of 0 percent interest for a set period.

Watch Out for Extra Fees: Cards can charge for all kinds of things—like late payments, cash advances, foreign purchases, or balance transfers. Depending on how you plan to use the card, these fees can add up fast. If you travel, for example, choose a card with no foreign transaction fees.

Look at Other Perks: Some cards come with extras like rental car insurance, roadside help, or extended warranties on things you buy. These can be great—but make sure you'll actually use them. If you won't, they're probably not worth paying more for (American Express 2025).

Once your card is approved, the real work begins—using it wisely.

One of the best practices for credit cards is to pay off your balance in full every month. Doing so helps you avoid interest charges entirely. It also shows lenders that you're responsible, which helps your credit score go up over time.

It's also important to know your credit limit—that's the maximum amount you're allowed to charge to your card. Stay well below that number. Most financial experts recommend keeping your balance under 30 percent of your credit limit (DeNicola 2023). If your card limit is $500, try not to carry more than $150 on it at any given time. Keeping your usage low helps boost your credit score and keeps you from falling into debt.

That said, credit cards can be risky if they're not used carefully. One of the most common problems? Letting your balance creep up slowly. Maybe it starts with a couple of small purchases—coffee here, snacks there—but suddenly, you've got a $300 bill you can't pay off. If you don't pay it all off, interest charges kick in, and the next month's balance is even higher.

To keep things under control, it helps to set your own monthly spending limit—and stick to it. Your card might let you spend $500, but that doesn't mean you should. Decide how much you can afford to pay back easily and make that your cap. Most credit card companies also offer payment reminders via text or email. These are a simple way to avoid late payments, which can damage your credit score. Even missing one due date can have a lasting impact, so it's worth setting up alerts the moment you activate your card.

If you ever feel like your balance is growing too fast, pause your spending. Leave the card at home for a few days, or remove it from your phone's digital wallet. Knowing when to slow down is part of being a responsible cardholder.

Eventually, good credit card habits pay off. You'll build a strong credit history, which opens up more financial opportunities in the future. Your first card is just the beginning. What matters most is how you manage it. With smart choices and clear limits, you can make credit work for you—not against you.

MANAGING CREDIT: HOW TO AVOID THE MOST COMMON MISTAKES

Credit can be super useful—but only if you handle it the right way. When it's misused, it can lead to serious stress, especially when the bills start piling up.

In the US, nearly half of credit card users—about 48 percent— carry a balance from month to month (Dickler 2025). That means they're not paying off their full bill each cycle, which adds up in interest and fees. For many people, this kind of debt isn't caused by big shopping sprees—it's often the result of unexpected emergencies, like car repairs or medical bills. That's why it's so important to learn how to stay on top of your credit early. Knowing what to watch out for can help you avoid the most common slipups.

One of the most common mistakes people make with credit is missing payments. It might not seem like a big deal to be a few days late, especially if you're waiting on your next paycheck. But even one missed due date can trigger late fees, hurt your credit score, and make it harder to qualify for better borrowing options in the future. Lenders and credit card companies want to know you can be trusted to pay back what you owe—and paying late sends the opposite message.

Another mistake? Opening too many credit accounts at once. You might think applying for a bunch of cards will give you more freedom to spend, but it often does more harm than good. Every time you apply, it creates a "hard inquiry" on your credit report. Too many inquiries can lower your score and make lenders wonder if you're in over your head. It can be tempting to accept every store card offer or sign up for multiple credit cards that promise rewards or bonuses. But these short-term perks aren't worth the long-term damage if they lead to debt or make it harder to manage your payments. A better approach is to apply for credit only when it makes sense—and when you know you can manage it responsibly.

To stay on track, set up automatic payments. Most banks and credit card companies give you the option to schedule payments in advance. You can choose to pay the minimum amount, your full balance, or a fixed amount every month. Scheduling your payments to line up with payday helps make sure your bill gets paid before you even think about spending the money elsewhere. This small step can take a lot of pressure off. You don't have to remember every due date or worry about forgetting a payment. And in time, your consistent payments will help build a strong credit history.

If you're thinking about applying for new credit, pause and ask yourself a few questions first:

- Do I need this credit, or am I just tempted by a sign-up bonus?
- Can I handle the payments easily?
- Will this account help me reach my financial goals?

Taking a moment to think before you apply can help you avoid extra fees, interest, and unnecessary stress.

The truth is that the effects of poor credit management can last a long time. A low credit score can lead to higher interest rates on loans, which means you end up paying more over time. It can also affect things like renting an apartment, buying a car, or qualifying for a mortgage later in life. Some employers even check credit history when hiring for certain jobs. So, while it might not seem urgent now, how you handle your credit today can affect your options years from now.

Building and maintaining good credit takes time, but it's absolutely within reach. Avoiding common traps like missed payments and unnecessary accounts is a strong start. From there, it's about being consistent, staying informed, and asking for help when you need it. With the right habits and tools, you can avoid the mistakes that hold others back—and keep moving forward toward your financial goals with confidence.

THE DEBT DEBATE: GOOD VS. BAD DEBT

The reality is that debt isn't always a bad thing. In fact, some types of debt can make it possible to reach goals that would otherwise be out of reach—like going to college or buying a car. What matters is how the debt works in your life: some can move you forward, while other kinds can slow you down or cause long-term stress.

Let's start with what's often called good debt. This is the kind of borrowing that supports your future. A common example is a student loan. Taking out a loan to pay for college or trade school can make sense because education can increase your chances of getting a higher-paying job. It's an investment in yourself. These loans usually come with lower interest rates and flexible repayment plans, which means they're easier to manage over time. Here are a few more examples:

Mortgage Loans: Buying a house usually means taking out a mortgage—a loan that's backed by the home itself. As you make payments, you gain more ownership (called equity) in the home. This can lead to more financial stability and may help build wealth in the future.

Business Loans: If you want to start a business, you might need to borrow money upfront. Loans or business credit lines can also help keep things running smoothly or support growth. If the business earns enough to support you (and maybe even employees), this kind of debt can be a smart move.

Interest-Free Loans: Some programs offer loans that don't charge interest at all, such as those for energyefficient home upgrades or down payment help when buying a house. Certain nonprofits also offer interest-free loans for students, small businesses, or people working to build credit.

Refinanced Debt: Replacing an old loan with a new one— like using a balance transfer credit card or a personal loan —can make monthly payments easier or reduce how much interest you pay.

People often do this to organize their debt or save money (DeNicola 2024; Fay 2024).

Now, let's talk about bad debt. This is the kind that doesn't give you anything valuable in return. High-interest credit card debt is one of the most common forms. It often builds up when people use credit for non-essential purchases like clothes, takeout, or entertainment—and then can't pay off the balance quickly. Because the interest adds up fast, you end up paying much more than the item was ever worth. Below are some other examples:

Payday Loans: These are short-term loans meant to cover expenses until your next paycheck. They're easy to get but come with huge fees—often $15 to $30 for every $100 borrowed. That adds up fast and translates to interest rates as high as 400 percent per year. Because of the high cost and short repayment window, payday loans can trap people in a cycle of debt.

Car Loans: Buying a car with a loan is sometimes necessary, but it's usually not the best kind of debt. Most cars lose value as soon as you drive them off the lot. While auto loan interest rates are usually lower than credit card rates, borrowing too much for a luxury vehicle can stretch your budget. It's smarter to choose a reliable, affordable car and pay the loan off on time.

Debt for Discretionary Spending: Using loans or credit to cover non-essential purchases—like vacations, designer items, hobbies, or other "wants"—can create long-term problems. These types of purchases don't build value, and the interest you'll pay adds unnecessary cost. If you can't afford it without borrowing, it might be better to save up and pay in cash later. As always, live within your means (DeNicola 2024; Fay 2024).

Knowing the difference between these types of debt can help you make smarter choices. Before taking on any debt, ask yourself:

- Is this going to help me reach a long-term goal?
- Will it increase my income or improve my quality of life in a meaningful way?
- Is it something I could save for instead of borrowing?

If the answer to those questions is no, it might be worth waiting or finding another way.

Not all borrowing opportunities are created equal. If you decide a loan is worth it, take a close look at the interest rate. That's the extra money you'll pay on top of what you borrow. Lower rates mean you pay less over time, so always compare offers if you have options.

You should also pay attention to the repayment terms. A longer term may sound easier because the monthly payments are lower, but you'll usually pay more in interest over time. A shorter term might be tougher each month, but it could save you money in the long run. Think about your current situation and your goals before choosing a loan plan.

If you're already dealing with bad debt, you're not stuck. There are ways to manage it and take back control. One method that works for a lot of people is called the debt snowball, where you focus on paying off your smallest debt first while making minimum payments on everything else. Once the smallest one is gone, you move on to the next. It's not just about math—it's about motivation. Paying off smaller amounts gives you momentum and helps you stay committed.

You can also try talking to your lender. It might feel intimidating, but many credit card companies are willing to lower your interest rate or adjust your payment plan if you're making an effort to pay consistently. These conversations can lead to smaller monthly payments and less interest over time.

SMART BORROWING: NAVIGATING STUDENT LOANS

Getting ready for college means making some big choices—and one of the biggest is figuring out how you're going to pay for it. College can lead to amazing opportunities, but it's no secret that it can be expensive. That's why a lot of students turn to loans to help cover things like tuition, textbooks, and living costs.

Student loans are a serious commitment, but they don't have to be scary—as long as you understand how they work and have a plan to manage them. Right now, student loan debt in the US is huge—more than $1.6 trillion in federal loans alone, with over 42 million people carrying some kind of student loan balance. So, if you end up needing to borrow, you're definitely not alone. The good news is that with the right knowledge and smart choices, you can take on college without letting debt take over your future. There are two main types of student loans: federal and private.

Federal student loans are offered through the US government and are usually the better option. They're divided into two categories:

- **Subsidized Loans:** Subsidized loans are for students with financial need. The government pays the interest on these while you're in school, during your grace period, and even during deferment.
- **Unsubsidized Loans:** Unsubsidized loans are available to most students, regardless of financial need. But here's the catch: Interest starts adding up as soon as the money is sent to your school—even while you're still in class.

Private loans, on the other hand, are offered by banks, credit unions, or other lenders. These should be your last resort. They often come with higher interest rates, stricter repayment terms, and fewer options if you're struggling to pay them back later. If you've hit the limit on federal loans and still need more help, make sure you fully understand what private lenders are offering before you sign anything.

How to Apply for a Student Loan

If you're planning to take out a federal student loan, your first step is to fill out the FAFSA—short for Free Application for Federal Student Aid. This form helps colleges and the government figure out how much financial help you qualify for.

You'll need to provide personal and financial details about yourself—and if you're still a dependent, your parent or guardian's info, too. Here's some of what you might need:

- Your FSA ID (this is your login for the FAFSA system) Social
- Security Number (or a registration number if you're not a US citizen)
- Tax forms, like W-2s and past income tax returns
- Bank and investment account info, if you have any (Cote 2023)

Once everything's submitted, the government will review your application and let you know how much money you're eligible to borrow. You'll also get a financial aid award letter from your school explaining what kinds of aid you've been offered, including loans, grants, or work-study.

Before accepting a loan, make sure you fully understand what you're signing up for—how much you're borrowing, when you'll need to start paying it back, and what your options are after graduation. Take your time reviewing them. It might be tempting to accept the full amount offered, but remember—you don't have to borrow everything. Only borrow what you really need to cover your education and living costs.

After graduation, you'll typically get a grace period—usually six months before your first payment is due (Federal Student Aid n.d.). That doesn't mean you should wait. If you can afford to make payments during that time, especially toward the interest, you'll save money in the long run.
When it's time to start making regular payments, look into income-driven repayment plans. These options adjust your monthly payments based on

how much money you're earning. They can make repayment feel less overwhelming, especially if you're starting out in an entry-level job. Some of these plans even forgive any remaining balance after twenty years, though you may owe taxes on the forgiven amount.

Staying on top of your loan payments has long-term benefits. Making consistent, on-time payments builds your credit history. That helps you later when you want to rent an apartment, get a car loan, or even qualify for better credit cards. A strong credit profile shows that you can handle money responsibly. But missing payments—or ignoring them—can lead to real trouble.

What Happens If You Don't Pay Back?

Falling behind on a student loan is serious—and defaulting (which usually means missing payments for a long time) can lead to a lot of problems beyond just being late.

Here's what can happen if you default on a federal student loan:

- You could be asked to pay the entire remaining loan balance right away.
- Your wages may be garnished, meaning money gets taken out of your paycheck automatically.
- In the future, your tax refunds or even Social Security benefits could be taken to repay the debt.
- You might get sued by the government or collection agency. You could be charged extra fees and collection costs on top of what you
- already owe.
- You'll lose access to future financial aid, including grants like the Pell Grant.
- You'll no longer qualify for deferment or forbearance, which are ways to pause payments if you're struggling. Your college may
- hold your transcripts or records, which could affect transferring schools or finishing your degree (Maher 2025).

The bottom line? Ignoring a loan doesn't make it go away—it makes things a lot harder. That's why it's so important to keep up with payments or ask for help if you're struggling. It's much easier to deal with problems early, so if you're ever having trouble making payments, talk to your loan servicer right away. They might be able to offer deferment or forbearance, which can temporarily pause your payments without the same harsh consequences.

Student loans don't have to hold you back as long as you approach them with a clear plan. Know what you're borrowing. Understand how the repayment process works. And always keep track of what you owe, even while you're still in school. You don't need to memorize every financial term or become a loan expert. You just need to stay informed, ask questions when you're unsure, and be proactive about your responsibilities.

MONEY SMARTS CHALLENGE: ARE YOU READY TO BORROW?

This chapter covered a lot—from credit scores and student loans to how your first swipe of a credit card can shape your financial future. Now it's your turn to think about how all of this connects to your life. What do I want

- my credit score to say about me one day? Am I ready for my first
- credit card—or do I still have more to learn? Do I know how to spot the difference between helpful and harmful debt?
- If I needed a loan for school, would I know where to start —and how to keep it under control?
- What's one habit I can build now that will help me with creditbuilding later?
-

You don't need to have all the answers yet. Just asking the right questions puts you in a better position than most. Because when you understand credit and borrowing, you're already planning for your life.

So, you've got the foundation down—budgeting, saving, and understanding credit. But beyond being careful with money, managing money is also about making smart moves with the money you keep. That's where investing comes in. In the next chapter, we'll break down how investing actually works, why you should start early, and how even small amounts can grow into something meaningful when you give them time. No stock market jargon, no boring lectures—just real talk about how to build a future that works for you.

5

INVESTING TO GROW YOUR MONEY FOR THE FUTURE

Saving is a smart move—but saving alone won't always get you where you want to go. That's where investing comes in. It's one of the best ways to help your money grow over time. Instead of just sitting in a bank account, your money has the chance to earn more by being put to work. A lot of teens think investing is only for adults or people who already have a lot of money. But that's not true. You don't have to be a financial expert—or even eighteen years old—to get started. In fact, the earlier you start, the better off you'll be later on.

So what is investing, really? Investing means using your money to buy something that has the potential to grow in value. As time goes by, that investment could earn you money through interest, dividends, or a rise in its overall value.

BEFORE YOU INVEST: LEARN THE BASICS

If you're thinking about jumping into investing, the first thing to do is learn the basics. You don't need to memorize complicated formulas, but you should understand a few core ideas:

- What types of investments exist? (Think stocks, bonds, mutual funds, ETFs.)
-

- What is risk tolerance? (How comfortable are you with the idea of losing money temporarily in exchange for the chance to earn more later?)
- What does diversification mean? (It's the idea of spreading your money across different investments so you're not relying on just one.)
- How does compounding work? (It's when the money you earn from investments starts earning its own money over time. That's how small investments can grow big.)

There are free resources all over the internet—including videos, apps, and even investment games—that can help you learn this stuff in a way that actually makes sense.

Set Your Goals Before You Start

It's easy to get excited about investing, but before putting your money anywhere, ask yourself why you're investing in the first place. Are you saving for something short-term, like a laptop or a car? Or are you thinking long-term, like college, a first home, or even early retirement?

Your goals will help you decide where to put your money. For short-term goals, you might be better off with a high-yield savings account. For longterm goals, investing can give your money more time to grow. Having clear goals also helps you stay focused and avoid getting caught up in short-term hype.

HOW TO START INVESTING AS A TEEN

While you don't need to be eighteen to invest, you will need a parent or guardian to help open an account. Here's how you can get started:

Choose the Right Type of Account

Since most investment platforms require users to be legal adults, you'll likely need a custodial account. This type of account is opened and managed by a parent or guardian, but the money belongs to you. Once you reach the age of majority (usually eighteen or twenty-one, depending on your state), the account transfers to your full control.

There are several types of custodial accounts:

- **UGMA and UTMA Accounts:** These are general-purpose accounts where the adult manages the investments until you come of age.
- **Custodial Roth IRAs:** These are great if you've earned income from a part-time job and want to invest for the long term, like retirement.
- **529 Plans:** They are designed specifically for education savings.

Some platforms—like Fidelity's Youth Account—are tailored for teens and don't require a minimum deposit. You can start investing with as little as one dollar, and many accounts allow you to buy fractional shares. That means you can own a piece of companies like Apple or Nike without buying an entire share.

Pick Investments That Make Sense for You

It's good to know how much risk you're comfortable with. Are you okay with the chance of losing money in exchange for the chance to earn more? Or do you prefer to play it safe and earn smaller returns? Once you've figured that out, you can check out different types of investments that match your comfort level and goals. Below are a few options.

Stocks (Also Called Shares)

When you buy a stock, you're buying a small piece of a company. If the company does well, your stock's value might go up. You can also earn money through dividends, which are small payments some companies give to shareholders from their profits.

Stock prices can go up and down depending on things like company news, market trends, and investor reactions. That means there's a chance to grow your money but also a chance to lose some—especially in the short term. Stocks are bought through stock exchanges, such as the New York Stock Exchange (NYSE) and NASDAQ, using trading apps or brokers. Other countries have their own stock exchanges, too.

So, how do you select stocks? Below is a guide from TeenVestor:

Talk to People You Know: Ask your parents, relatives, neighbors, or family friends about the companies they work for (if they're not government employees). They might give you a behind-thescenes look at how a business is doing or share info about exciting new products. Just remember—they can't legally share confidential insider info.

Follow Your Interests and Hobbies: Think about what you enjoy—sports, gaming, fashion, tech, or music. If there's a brand or product you love, find out who makes it. Chances are, that company may be publicly traded. It's easier to stay curious about a company when you already care about what it does.

Pay Attention to What Your Friends Like: Notice what's trending at school or among your friends. Are certain snacks, drinks, shoes, or apps super popular? Sometimes, the things everyone uses can point to companies that are worth researching.

Read Business News: You don't need to read full articles every day, but checking sites like Yahoo! Finance, MarketWatch, or CNBC's teenfriendly content can keep you updated on big companies, market trends, and what's happening in industries that interest you.

Explore Companies Based in Your Area: Look up major companies headquartered in your state. You might even know someone who works there. Use business rankings (like the Fortune 500) to see which local companies are making a national impact.

Avoid Social Media Stocks: Just because someone sounds confident online doesn't mean their advice is trustworthy. Some people use social media to hype up stocks for personal gain, and following their lead could get you into legal trouble—especially if insider info is involved (TeenVestor n.d.).

Exchange-Traded Funds (ETFs)

ETFs are like a bundle of different investments (such as stocks, bonds, or both) rolled into one. Instead of buying one company's stock, you're buying a slice of many. This spreads out your risk and can make investing less stressful.

Some ETFs follow certain themes—like tech stocks or international companies—while others track big market indexes like the ASX 200. They're easy to buy through the same platforms that offer regular stocks and are known for being low-cost and easy to manage.

Here are a few smart tips to take to make sure investing in ETFs fits your goals:

- **Know Your Time Frame**
  - Ask yourself: When will I need this money? If you're investing for something far in the future—like retirement—you've got a long time to let your investments grow. That means you can afford to take more risks. If your goal is closer (like buying a car in a few years), you might want to be more cautious.
- **Understand How Much Risk You're Okay With** Some people
  - are fine seeing their investments go up and down in value, while others get nervous when prices drop. Again, this is called risk tolerance. If you're okay with ups and downs for the chance of bigger rewards, you're probably more aggressive. If you want a balance between risk and stability,

you're likely moderate. If you like to play it safe and avoid big swings, you're more conservative.

Many investment apps and websites offer short quizzes to help you figure out your comfort level with risk. A quick internet search can give you a list.

- **Pick Your Mix of Investments**
  - Your asset mix is how you divide your money between different types of investments like stocks, bonds, or cash.
    - **Aggressive Mix:** Mostly stocks (around 70 to 90 percent), with fewer bonds
    - **Moderate Mix:** More balanced between stocks and bonds
    - **Conservative Mix:** Heavier on bonds and cash, with fewer stocks

If you're young and don't need the money soon, you can usually take on more risk with a stock-heavy mix.

- **Choose the Types of ETFs**
  - Now that you know your goals and risk level, you can look at different kinds of ETFs. Some popular categories include:
    - **By Company Size (Market Cap):** Large, mid, or small companies
    - **Growth ETFs:** Focused on fast-growing companies
    - **Dividend ETFs:** Made up of companies that pay out regular profits (called dividends)
    - **Geographic ETFs:** Focused on companies from a certain country or region (like the U.S., Europe, or Asia)
    - **Sector ETFs:** Focused on specific industries like tech, health, or energy
- **Pick the ETFs That Fit You Best**
  - Once you know the type of ETF you want, compare a few options. Here are some things to look for:
    - **Expense Ratio:** This is the fee the ETF charges. Lower is better—it leaves more money in your pocket.
    - **Assets Under Management:** Bigger ETFs usually trade more often, which makes it easier to buy or sell.

- **Dividend Yield:** If you want regular payouts, check how much the ETF returns through dividends. **Performance**
- **History:** Older ETFs with a longer track record give you more data to see how they've performed.

Tracking Accuracy: Some ETFs don't follow their benchmarks very closely. Look for ones that match their index with only small differences (Thune n.d.).

ETFs can be a smart and simple way to start investing, especially when you understand your goals and choose carefully. With the right mix of research and patience, you can build a strong portfolio that grows with you.

Bonds

Bonds are loans you give to companies or the government. In return, they agree to pay you back later—with interest. Bonds are usually seen as a safer investment than stocks, but the returns are smaller. There are many types of bonds, and each comes with different levels of risk, reward, and timeframes (short, medium, or long-term). Here are some of the most common ones:

US Treasury Bonds: These bonds are issued by the federal government and are known for being extremely safe. They're backed by the US government, so the risk of losing money is very low. Investors often use them as a benchmark to compare other bonds. You can even buy them directly from the government at TreasuryDirect.gov.

Corporate Bonds: These are bonds issued by companies to raise money. Since businesses can sometimes fail or face financial issues, these bonds carry more risk than government bonds. The level of risk (and reward) depends on how stable the company is. Credit rating agencies like Moody's or S&P give grades to help investors judge how reliable each company is when it comes to repaying debt. **Mortgage Bonds:** Mortgage bonds are backed by home loans. When people make mortgage payments, that money is used to pay the bondholders. Some are guaranteed by the government (like Ginnie Mae bonds), while others are issued by large financial companies and carry more risk. These bonds are also affected by changes in interest rates because people might refinance their loans when rates drop.

High-Yield Bonds: Also known as "junk bonds," these come from companies with lower credit ratings. They offer higher interest rates to make up for the extra risk. These can be tempting, but they're not always the best fit for new investors.

Municipal Bonds (Muni Bonds): These are issued by cities, states, or other local governments to fund public projects like schools or roads. Many muni bonds are taxfree, meaning you won't have to pay federal taxes on the interest you earn.

Foreign and Emerging Market Bonds: These are issued by other countries or companies based outside the US. Bonds from developing nations (called "emerging markets") usually pay higher interest but also come with political and currency risks (Bromberg 2025).

Some bonds are hard to get into because they require big amounts of money upfront. But don't worry—many ETFs include bonds, so you can still get exposure without needing thousands of dollars. **Micro-Investing Apps**

Apps like Raiz and Spaceship let you start investing with just your spare change. For example, if you buy a snack for $2.60, the app might round it up to $3 and invest the extra 40 cents for you. Other famous micro-investing apps include:

- Webull
- Robinhood
- Interactive Brokers
- Stash
- Sofi (White 2024)

These apps are super convenient and designed for people who are just getting started. However, they charge fees—either monthly or as a percentage of your investments—which can cost more than other options over time. Also, you don't directly own the investments—the app does on your behalf—so it's different from buying stocks or ETFs in your own name.

Real Estate Investment Trusts (REITs)

Interested in real estate but don't have hundreds of thousands to buy property? REITs are companies that invest in buildings like shopping centers or apartment blocks. When you buy shares in a REIT, you're basically owning a small part of that real estate. REITs pay out money from rent and property sales as dividends, so they can be a solid way to earn income and invest in property— without having to be a landlord.

There are different types of REITs, namely:

Retail REITs: These REITs invest in shopping centers, malls, and other retail spaces. They make money by renting out space to stores. But if the stores aren't doing well and can't pay rent, these REITs can take a hit. Strong tenants—like grocery chains or hardware stores— are more reliable. Also, because online shopping is growing, some retail REITs are trying to fill their spaces with offices or services instead of stores.

Residential REITs: Residential REITs focus on apartment buildings and other rental housing. These tend to do well in cities where buying a home is super expensive, like New York or LA. When more people move to an area for jobs, demand for apartments goes up, which means higher rents. The best-performing residential REITs are usually the ones in cities with growing populations and strong economies.

Healthcare REITs: These REITs own properties like hospitals, clinics, nursing homes, and retirement centers. As the population ages and more people need care, the demand for these properties may grow. Good healthcare REITs spread their investments across different kinds of facilities and locations. It's also important that they work with reliable healthcare providers and have strong financial backing.

Office REITs: Office REITs invest in buildings used for business. Their income comes from long-term leases with companies. These REITs are more likely to succeed in cities with strong job markets and low unemployment. When looking at office REITs, it helps to focus on those with properties in busy economic areas and enough funding to expand or upgrade their buildings.

Mortgage REITs: Instead of owning buildings, mortgage REITs invest in home loans and mortgage-backed securities. They earn money from the interest on these loans. But they're also more sensitive to changes in interest rates—if rates go up, their value can drop. These REITs often borrow money to invest, so if borrowing becomes more expensive, it can hurt their profits.

Again, you don't need to put all your money in at once. Try starting with a small amount and get comfortable watching how the market moves. You'll learn a lot just by being involved.

Monitor and Adjust

As you gain more experience, you'll want to check in on your portfolio from time to time. Investing isn't something you set and forget forever. Markets go up and down, and your goals might change, too. Review your investments regularly, especially if you're planning to invest long-term. Soon, you will get better at making decisions that fit your personal financial goals.

Starting early gives you a serious advantage, even if you're only working with small amounts. With time, consistency, and a little patience, your money can grow in ways that a regular savings account just can't match. The magic behind it is compound interest, which the great Albert Einstein referred to as "the eighth wonder of the world" (Downie 2024).

THE POWER OF COMPOUND INTEREST

Think of compound interest as planting money seeds that keep multiplying. At first, your investment grows slowly—like a tiny sprout. But soon, it grows into a tree that produces more seeds, and those seeds grow into even more trees. Eventually, your money earns more money all on its own—

even while you're sleeping. That's the magic of compounding: Your growth builds on itself and just keeps going.

So, how does it differ from simple interest? Simple interest is calculated only on the money you originally invested (called the principal). Compound interest builds on the principal and the interest you've already earned. It's like getting paid for money you didn't even have to work for. The more often your interest is added—whether it's yearly, monthly, or daily—the faster your money grows. And the longer you leave it untouched, the more dramatic the results.

Let's say you invest $1,000 at a 5 percent annual interest rate:

- With simple interest, after ten years, you earn $500. Your total is $1,500.
- With compound interest (compounded yearly), after ten years, your total is about $1,629. That's an extra $129 just from compounding.

If you leave it for twenty years instead of ten, your $1,000 could grow to about $2,653 without adding anything extra. Here's another example:

If you invest $100 a month into an account that earns 6 percent interest yearly, here's what could happen:

- After ten years, you've contributed $12,000—but your account might be worth about $16,470.
- After twenty years, it could grow to around $44,000. After thirty
- years, you're looking at almost $100,000—just from investing consistently and letting interest do its thing.

See the logic? The earlier you start, the more time your money has to grow. You don't need a lot of cash or complex strategies—just consistency, patience, and time. Compound interest does the heavy lifting—you just have to start.

INVESTING WITH PURPOSE

What if your money could grow and make a positive impact at the same time? That's the idea behind ethical investing—putting your cash into companies and funds that reflect your values. It's not just about earning returns; it's about supporting causes you care about through smart financial choices.

Ethical investing is sometimes called socially responsible investing (SRI), and it's all about choosing investments that do more than just make money. These investments often follow ESG standards —that stands for Environmental, Social, and Governance. In other words, they look at how companies:

- Care for the planet
- Treat their workers and communities
- Run their businesses fairly and transparently

If you care about climate change, equal rights, clean energy, or companies that treat their employees well, ethical investing gives you the chance to support those values with your wallet.

Ethical investing gives you more control over the kind of impact your money makes. When more people demand better behavior from companies, it sends a strong message. That pressure encourages businesses to treat people better, reduce harm to the environment, and stay honest in how they operate. Of course, it's important to remember that ethical investments may not always grow as quickly as some traditional ones—but many do just fine. Plenty of socially responsible funds have performed well while sticking to strong standards. So you don't have to feel like you're giving up financial growth to support what matters to you.

Finding investments that match your values takes some research, but there are tools to help. Start by looking for companies or funds that focus on ESG factors. Many financial apps and websites now include ESG scores, which show how a company stacks up on things like sustainability, diversity, and transparency. Organizations like MSCI ESG Research, Sustainalytics, and

FTSE Russell give ESG scores and reports on companies. These are a great place to start your research.

You can also look into companies that talk openly about their efforts—like reducing pollution, helping their communities, or building inclusive workplaces. If you're not sure where to begin, look at funds that are already built with social responsibility in mind. But be careful of conflicting connections. Some companies in ethical funds have ties to businesses that raise ethical concerns.

For example:

> Woolworths is in many ethical funds, yet it owns a major share in Endeavour Group, which operates thousands of slot machines—more than some casinos.
>
> Tesla might seem like an obvious ethical choice because of its electric cars, but it was once removed from the S&P 500 ESG index while some oil companies stayed on (Matthews 2023).

So, what are examples of ethical investments? Here are some wellknown firms making a real impact through ESG investing.

- BlackRock
    - **Assets Under Management:** $10 trillion (2023)
    - **CEO:** Larry Fink
    - BlackRock is the biggest investment manager in the world and takes ESG investing seriously. It plans to have 75 percent of its investments supporting businesses that are working to cut greenhouse gas emissions by 2030. BlackRock also combines environmental and social goals in its strategies, aiming to support both the planet and communities.
- Vanguard
    - **Assets Under Management:** $9.3 trillion (2024)
    - **CEO:** Salim Ramji
    -

Vanguard offers a range of ESG investment options, including funds that avoid fossil fuels, tobacco, and weapons. It also runs active ESG funds that support companies that show strong or improved sustainability practices. Vanguard doesn't take a one-size-fits-all approach—it tailors solutions to fit different investor goals.

- State Street Global Advisors
  - **Assets Under Management:** $4.1 trillion (2023)
  - **CEO:** Yie-Hsin Hung
  - State Street has been involved in sustainable investing for a long time. Its focus includes improving how companies are managed and ensuring transparency for shareholders. The firm has pledged to invest $750 billion in sustainable finance by 2030.
- Fidelity Investments
  - **Assets Under Management:** $4.9 trillion (2023)
  - **CEO:** Abigail Johnson
  - Fidelity includes ESG analysis in its actively managed funds, meaning they research companies deeply before investing. Their sustainable investing team looks at environmental risks, social responsibility, and corporate governance with the same seriousness as any other financial factor.
- J.P. Morgan
  - **Assets Under Management:** $2.9 trillion (2023)
  - **CEO:** Jamie Dimon
  - J.P. Morgan has committed to supporting $2.5 trillion in climate and sustainability projects by 2033. They offer several sustainable investing options and aim to back projects that support economic growth in fair, inclusive ways (Jessen 2024).

Now that you know which big-name firms are leading the charge in ethical investing, it's time to figure out how *you* can get started. Choosing where to put your money is making sure your investments reflect what you care about most. Use the checklist below to help guide your next steps.

Know what matters to you. Is it clean energy? Human rights? Animal welfare? Make a list of causes you care about most.

Check ESG ratings. Use websites or investment apps to see how companies or funds score on environmental, social, and governance issues.

Mix it up. Don't put everything in one place—build a portfolio with a variety of socially responsible options.

Stay on top of it. Companies change, and so do your goals. Review your investments now and then to make sure they still match what you believe in.

Investing isn't something you just set and forget. As companies shift and your values grow, it's important to check in on your investments and make sure they still align with what matters to you. Now that you've learned the basics, it's your turn to put it into action with this challenge.

MONEY SMARTS CHALLENGE: DESIGN YOUR FIRST INVESTMENT PLAN

Grab a notebook or open the notes app on your phone. Answer these questions honestly:

- What's one or two goals you want to hit by investing— something that matters to you?
- How much can you realistically start with—even if it's just $10? What kind of investment are you curious to try? Stocks?
- Index funds? Something else? How long are you willing to let your money sit and grow?
- Your answers don't have to be perfect or final. This is your starter plan—a way to turn what you've learned into action. Update it as you go, and watch how your knowledge (and confidence) grows along with your money.

Once you've started building your investment plan, you're already thinking ahead—and that's a big deal. But money management isn't standing still. The financial world is changing fast, and the way people earn, save, spend, and invest is evolving with it. In the next chapter, we'll dive into some of the most popular modern money trends.

6

MODERN FINANCIAL TRENDS

Money moves fast now—faster than ever. You don't have to step inside a bank, fill out paperwork, or wait days to cash a check. With just a phone, you can get paid, send cash, invest, save, or even start a mini business—all before lunch. From digital banking and crypto to gig apps and side hustles, today's money game doesn't play by the old rules. And if you want to stay ahead, you don't need to memorize financial jargon—you just need to know what tools are out there and how to use them wisely. This chapter is your guide to the now. The tech, the trends, and the real-world ways you can earn, manage, and grow your money—on your terms.

BANKING ON THE GO

It's Saturday morning, and instead of running to the bank or waiting in line, you're checking your balance or depositing a check right from your phone. For millions of people—this isn't just convenient. It's normal. Digital banking has officially taken over.

As of now, there are about 1.75 billion digital banking users worldwide that are processing $2.7 million worth of transactions every minute (Schwarz 2024). That's not a fad—it's how modern banking works. Mobile apps, online-only banks, and instant transfers are replacing paper statements and in-person visits. And for digital natives like you, this kind of access fits perfectly into your lifestyle.

How to Choose the Right Digital Bank

With so many options out there, picking the right online bank takes a little research. Here are a few things you should look for:

FDIC Insurance: This is nonnegotiable. If a bank is insured by the FDIC, your money is protected up to $250,000—even if the bank goes under. You can verify this at the FDIC's website.

High Interest Rates: Some online banks offer much better returns on savings than traditional ones. For example, $5,000 in a savings account earning 1.15 percent over five years earns a lot more than the same amount in an account that pays only 0.1 percent. The difference adds up, especially when you leave the money alone.

Low or No Fees: Look for banks that don't charge monthly maintenance fees or require big minimum balances. Banks like Ally, Capital One, and Marcus by Goldman Sachs offer savings accounts with no fees and no penalties for low balances.

Huge ATM Networks: Need cash? Many online banks are part of networks like Allpoint or MoneyPass, which offer tens of thousands of ATMs nationwide. Some banks even refund ATM fees if you use machines outside their network.

Responsive Customer Service: Since there's no physical branch, good support matters. Some banks offer 24/7 phone lines, online chat, or even secure messaging within their apps. If you ever run into a problem, you'll want help that's easy to reach.

Built-In Money Tools: Many online banks let you organize your savings into "buckets" for specific goals— like saving for a concert, college, or your first car. Some even let you link accounts from other banks so you can see your full financial picture in one place.

User-Friendly Apps: A solid mobile app should let you do everything from transferring money to depositing checks. You should also be able to open new accounts, send money to friends, and manage bills—all from your phone (Bennett 2022).

With convenience comes responsibility. Make sure your accounts are protected. Turn on two-factor authentication so your login requires a code sent to your phone or email. Don't reuse passwords, and update them regularly. Watch out for phishing scams— messages pretending to be from your bank that try to steal your info. Never click sketchy links or give out your password.

Digital banking is fast, flexible, and designed to keep up with your life. It puts your financial tools in your pocket and lets you make smart moves on your own schedule. As you explore apps and online banks, remember that you're using technology to manage your money.

WHAT YOU SHOULD KNOW ABOUT CRYPTOCURRENCY, BITCOIN, AND BEYOND

You've probably heard people talking about Bitcoin or crypto as if it's the future of money—and in some ways, it kind of is. Cryptocurrency is a type of money that lives completely online. There are no bills or coins, and no government or central bank is behind it. Instead, it runs on a special kind of technology built to be secure, transparent, and hard to mess with.

At the center of it all is something called blockchain—a public record of every crypto transaction that happens. You could say that it's a giant digital notebook shared across thousands of computers around the world. Once a transaction is added, it can't be changed. This setup helps keep things honest and avoids the need for a middleman like a bank.

So how does this all work in real life? Let's take a look at two of most wellknown cryptocurrencies and what makes them different: Bitcoin and Ethereum.

Bitcoin was the first cryptocurrency created in 2009, and it's still the most well-known. People sometimes call it "digital gold" because it's often used as a way to store value (Laboure n.d.). What makes it unique is that there will only ever be 21 million Bitcoins. That limited supply is part of what makes people want to own it.

Then there's Ethereum, which works a little differently. While Bitcoin is mainly used like money, Ethereum is more like a giant digital building platform. Developers use it to create smart contracts—agreements written directly into code. These contracts run themselves once certain conditions are met without needing someone to oversee them. Apps built on Ethereum are used for everything from digital art sales to decentralized finance.

Other popular cryptocurrency coins include:

Tether (USDT): Tether is a type of stablecoin, which means its value is tied to the US dollar. It's mainly used for trading and transferring money quickly without big price swings.

XRP (XRP): Created by Ripple, XRP is designed for fast, low-cost money transfers across borders. It's used by some financial institutions as a way to move money efficiently.

BNB (BNB): BNB was launched by Binance, one of the largest crypto exchanges in the world. It's used to pay for trading fees on the platform and for transactions in the Binance ecosystem.

Solana (SOL): Solana is known for super-fast transaction speeds and low fees. It's popular for decentralized apps, games, and NFTs (digital collectibles).

USD Coin (USDC): Like Tether, USDC is a stablecoin tied to the US dollar. It's used mostly for safe, steady transactions and is backed by real-world reserves.

Dogecoin (DOGE): Dogecoin started as a joke, but it gained popularity thanks to memes and internet culture. Today, it's often used for tipping, donations, and small online payments (Jacoby 2025).

If you're interested in buying crypto, you'll need to use an exchange—a website or app where you can swap your regular money (like dollars) for cryptocurrency. Popular platforms include Coinbase, Kraken, and

Binance.US. They make it pretty easy to create an account, connect your bank info, and start buying.

Once you own crypto, the next step is figuring out how to keep it safe. Crypto lives in something called a wallet. Some wallets are apps on your phone (hot wallets), while others are physical devices (cold wallets). A cold wallet looks like a USB stick, and it stores your coins offline, making it much harder for hackers to access. If you're serious about holding crypto long-term, storing it offline is often the safer option.

Cryptocurrency has some major benefits. For starters, it's fast. You can send money across the world in minutes without needing a bank to approve the transaction. It can also be helpful for people who don't have access to traditional banking. But here's the thing —crypto also comes with risk. Prices can swing wildly in a short time. One day, a coin might be worth $100; the next, it could drop to $40. That kind of unpredictability makes it a risky investment, especially if you're putting in money you can't afford to lose. There's also the legal side. Different countries have different rules when it comes to crypto. In some places, it's accepted. In others, it's restricted or even banned. Laws are still catching up, so it's important to stay updated before diving in too deep.

If you're curious about cryptocurrency, that's a good thing. Just remember— it's not a shortcut to wealth. It's a tool, and like any tool, you need to know how to use it properly. Start by learning the basics. Follow updates from trusted sources, such as CoinDesk, U.Today, Decrypt, Bankless, BeinCrypto, and The Block (Brooks n.d.). And don't put money into crypto unless you fully understand what you're getting into!

For teens especially, this is a chance to explore new tech and learn financial responsibility at the same time. Crypto might become a bigger part of the future—but understanding it now helps you make smarter choices later so that you can avoid potential losses. Consider the experience of Ethan Nguonly, a twenty-two-year-old software engineer from Orange County, California. Between November 2021 and June 2022, Ethan lost approximately $80,000 by investing in crypto on margin. His losses included $30,000 of his original investment and about $50,000 in unrealized gains. Ethan initially invested around $40,000 in Bitcoin and Ethereum, along with a few hundred dollars in altcoins like Shiba Inu and Dogecoin. As Bitcoin's price surged, he decided to buy more— about $15,000 worth— using borrowed funds. At one point, Ethan was up about $50,000 as Bitcoin reached its all-time high. However, by the summer of 2022, the crypto market had declined significantly, leading to substantial losses. Reflecting on his experience, Ethan admitted, "I was investing with some money that I didn't necessarily have." (McNair 2023).

MAKING MONEY YOUR WAY: SIDE HUSTLES AND THE GIG LIFE

Want to make your own money doing something you actually enjoy—or at least something that fits around your schedule? You don't need a full-time job or a business degree to start earning. Thanks to side hustles and the gig economy, you can tap into real opportunities to earn cash, build skills, and explore what you're good at—all while keeping school a priority.

A side hustle is anything you do outside of school (or another job) to earn extra income. Maybe you walk dogs in your neighborhood, sell custom jewelry online, or design logos for local businesses. These projects can be fun and flexible and even lead to something bigger if you stick with them.

The gig economy is a little different. It's built around short-term or flexible jobs—like delivering food, running errands, or doing freelance work online. You pick your gigs, set your hours, and decide how much you want to take on. For teens juggling school, sports, or other responsibilities, this flexibility is a major win.

Where to Start: Hustles That Fit You

Not sure where to begin? Start with what you're good at or what you already enjoy doing in your free time. Maybe you're great with animals—try offering pet-sitting or dog-walking services for neighbors. If you're the goto person when your friends need homework help, consider tutoring younger students. Good with younger kids? Babysitting is always in demand, especially for parents who need a night out or weekend help. If you're handy with tools, offer to assemble furniture, help with minor yard work, or assist neighbors with small repairs. If you're organized and reliable, helping someone move or clean out their garage could turn into a regular gig. If you're into sports or fitness, some families might pay for informal sports coaching or basic training support for younger kids—especially if you've played a sport for years and know how to teach the basics. And if you're into baking, crafting, or making handmade items, consider selling your goods at school events, community markets, or pop-ups.

The trick is to match your skills to what people around you need— and then let them know you're available. Small jobs can grow fast once people know you're dependable.

If you don't prefer a physical job, here are some popular (and practical) ways to make money from your laptop or phone:

Data Entry Clerk: If you're fast on the keyboard and detail-oriented, data entry might be a great fit. You'll help companies organize info into spreadsheets or databases. Some jobs have age minimums (like sixteen or eighteen), so double-check before applying.

Freelance Graphic Designer: You don't have to wait to go to art school to start designing. If you enjoy creating with tools like Canva, Photoshop, or Illustrator, offer your skills to local clubs, student groups, or small businesses. Build a portfolio, and you'll be ready for paying clients in no time. **Freelance Video Editor:** If you've got an eye for pacing, music, and storytelling, try editing videos. Whether it's YouTube intros, birthday montages, or school project recaps, people are always looking for help with editing.

You'll need some basic software and a few sample projects to get started.

Virtual Assistant: Being organized and reliable can actually make you money. Virtual assistants help with scheduling, emailing, researching, or booking appointments. If you're someone who loves crossing things off a to-do list, this might be your thing.

Freelance Content Writer: Does writing come naturally to you? Turn it into income by writing blogs, product descriptions, or website content. Businesses pay per article or word, so if you can write clearly, edit well, and meet deadlines, this one's worth exploring.

Online Tutor: If you've mastered a subject—or you're just really good at explaining things—offer tutoring. Some platforms require you to be eighteen, but others allow teens to help their peers. Bonus: You get better at the subject, too.

Sell Your Stuff Online: Are you crafty or have cool stuff you no longer need? Set up shop on sites like Etsy or Depop. You can sell handmade goods or resell clothes and accessories. It's a great way to learn basic business skills like pricing, shipping, and customer service.

Start a YouTube Channel: Into gaming, fashion, comedy, or tutorials? Start recording and posting. If you stay consistent, build a following, and keep learning, you could monetize through ads, sponsorships, or selling merch. Just make sure to follow platform rules, especially around age and content.

Take Surveys and Give Feedback: Some sites will pay for your opinion on ads, products, or websites. The pay is usually low, but it's low-effort too. Set up a separate email and stick with legit platforms to stay safe.

Try Quick Online Gigs: Have ten spare minutes? Some websites pay for micro-tasks like watching videos, testing websites, or doing simple research. These short jobs add up—especially if you're efficient and do a few at a time (Birt 2024).

Making It Work Around School

Balancing a hustle with your class schedule can be tricky, but it's doable if you stay organized. Start by picking times that work best for you—like weekends or late afternoons—and be honest about how many hours you can really commit each week. Don't burn yourself out. School comes first, so think of your hustle as something that fits around your priorities, not something that takes over. Bonus: Managing your time now builds habits that'll seriously pay off later, no matter what path you take.

What to Know Before You Jump In

Finding a side hustle that fits your skills is only half the equation. The other half is making sure it doesn't interfere with everything else going on in your life—especially school. Homework, tests, sports, and family time don't disappear just because you've started earning money. Gig and side hustle work is flexible—but it also comes with a few responsibilities. Unlike a regular job, most gigs don't include things like health benefits or automatic tax withholding. That means you'll need to keep track of what you earn and save for taxes if you cross income thresholds. (Tip: Using a simple budgeting app can help.)

Another heads-up: Income can be unpredictable. Some weeks might be packed with opportunities, while others are slow. If you're relying on that money for something important, it's smart to build in a cushion.

Standout Tips for Teen Hustlers

Once you've picked your side hustle and figured out how to balance it with school, the next step is leveling up. A few small moves can make a huge difference in how much you earn, how many clients you get, and how long you stay motivated. If you want to stand out in a crowded crowd of teen hustlers, these tips can help you work smarter—not just harder.

Promote Yourself Online: Use Instagram, TikTok, or a simple website to show your work and attract new customers.

Network in Real Life: Ask friends, family, or neighbors if they know anyone who needs your skills. Word-of-mouth still works.

Mix It Up. Try more than one platform or gig. If you're tutoring, maybe also sell printables on Etsy or offer résumé help to classmates.

Time It Right: Delivery drivers can earn more during meal times.

Freelancers should stay aware of client deadlines.

Sure, the extra cash is great—but there's more to it than that. Every side hustle or gig helps you build real-world skills: time management, customer service, communication, and problem-solving. You're not just earning—you're learning how to take charge of your own work and find your own rhythm. Whether you're building a small business, trying different gigs, or just exploring your options, this experience adds to your confidence, your résumé, and maybe even your future career path.

MONEY SMARTS CHALLENGE: ARE YOU FINANCIALLY FUTURE-READY?

Technology is changing the way money moves—and fast. Digital banking, crypto, and side hustles are becoming part of everyday life for teens just like you. So now it's your turn to reflect:

- What role does technology already play in how you handle money? If you could start a side hustle today, what would it be—
- and how would you make it work with your schedule? Would you feel confident using a digital bank or investing through an app?
- Why or why not?
  Do you see cryptocurrency as an opportunity, a risk, or both?
- What would you need to learn before jumping in? What's one tool, platform, or app you're curious to explore more after reading this
- chapter?

Take your time to answer these questions in a journal, notes app, or even a voice memo. Think of this as your personal blueprint for how you want to use tech to grow your money, not just keep up with trends.

Technology, side hustles, and new ways to manage money are changing how we think about earning and spending. But knowing the tools is only half the story. The other half? It's all in your mindset. How you feel about money, how you handle pressure, and what really motivates you can shape your entire financial future. That's why, in this next chapter, we're slowing down to focus on your relationship with money—from your goals to your fears and everything in between.

7

MONEY AND MINDSET

It's easy to feel stuck when thinking about your financial future. Maybe you've got big dreams—like getting your own car, going to college, or starting a business—but no idea how to get there. Or maybe you're afraid of messing up, so you don't start at all. That hesitation is totally normal. In fact, lots of people avoid setting money goals because they're scared of falling short or don't know where to begin.

But here's something to keep in mind: 83 percent of people who set financial goals say they feel better about their money within a year (Borghesan n.d.). Not because they nailed every goal perfectly, but because they took action— and that made all the difference.

This chapter is here to help you do the same. We'll break down how to set goals that actually mean something to you, how to build a plan you can stick with, and how to face the fears that try to slow you down. Reaching your goals isn't about being fearless—it's about moving forward anyway.

HOW TO SET GOALS AND DREAM BIG

Summer break is just around the corner. You've got big plans: maybe it's concerts, road trips, or a few lazy beach days. But when you check your wallet or bank balance, those plans suddenly feel a little out of reach. That sting? It's not just about money—it's about *not having a plan* for the money. And the truth is that financial goals are your secret to making those plans real.

Setting goals might sound like an adult thing to do, but it's actually a simple way to make sure your future self gets to enjoy the life you want—without stressing every time you spend. Here's a simple guide to help you in the process.

- **Finding Your "Why"**
    - Before you pick a number or set a savings goal, take a second to ask yourself this: Why do I want to do this? Maybe you want an emergency fund so you're not stuck if your phone breaks or your job hours get cut. Or you're trying to save for college to ease the pressure on your future self—or your parents.

    Attaching a reason to a goal makes it real. Instead of "I want money," it becomes "I want enough to cover rent next year" or "I don't want to rely on credit cards for emergencies." When you know why you're doing something, you're way more likely to stick with it.
- **Short-Term vs. Long-Term Goals**
    - Short-term goals are things you want to make happen soon—within a few months or a couple of years. That could mean saving for a new laptop, building a $500 emergency fund, or buying concert tickets. Long-term goals are the bigger ones that take time.

    Think college tuition, a first car, or even retirement (yes, it's far away—but starting early makes it way easier).
- **Take a Look at Where You Are**
    - Not sure how much you can save or where to begin?

Start by figuring out your current situation. How much do you earn from allowance, side hustles, or part-time work? Do you have regular expenses, like a phone bill,

- school supplies, or gas money? Are you already saving anything?
- Do you have a budget—or a rough idea of where your money goes? Having this info helps you plan smarter.
- **SMART Goal-Setting**
- Now that you've got a sense of your situation, it's time to set a goal that you can stick with. Use the SMART system to guide you:
- Specific – What are you saving for?
- Measurable – How much do you need?
- Achievable – Can you realistically hit this goal? Realistic – Are
- you pushing yourself without setting yourself up to fail? Time-bound – What's your deadline?
- Let's say you want to save $300 for a trip with friends. Your goal might look like this:
- "I want to save S300 by June 1. I'll set aside $25 a week from my paycheck and cut back on fast food." That's clear. You can track
- it. And it gives you a finish line.

- **Write It Down (Seriously)**
  - This step might feel small, but it matters: Write your goal down. Use a journal, a budgeting app, or even a sticky note on your mirror. When your goal lives somewhere outside your head, it's easier to stay focused —and way harder to forget.

Goals aren't set in stone. Life happens—maybe you land a new gig that helps you save faster. Or maybe an emergency pops up, and you need to pause your savings for a while. That doesn't mean you failed. Adjust your timeline, tweak your target, and keep going. You don't need to be perfect to succeed. You just have to always show up for your goals, even when things get messy.

Big goals take time. So, while you're working your way there, give yourself credit for showing up. Hit a mini goal? Celebrate with something simple: a treat, a day off from spending, or just hyping yourself up. These little wins keep you motivated—and make the process more fun. Once you knock out major goals, feel free to dream bigger. Maybe you'll start investing, launch a small business, or plan a future move. Your goals grow with you.

FACING FOMO AND FINANCIAL FREAKOUTS

Money can mess with your head. Scrolling through social media and seeing people flexing vacations, new clothes, or the "perfect" lifestyle can make you feel like you're falling behind. If you've ever stressed over money, felt pressured to keep up, or worried you're not doing enough, you're not alone.

How to Deal with Money Stress and the Fear of Falling Behind

Seeing your friends post about new sneakers, weekend getaways, or concert tickets can trigger a little voice in your head: "Should I be doing that too?" That feeling has a name—Financial FOMO (Fear of Missing Out)—and it's more common than you think. Maybe you've skipped your budget to join a last-minute dinner or bought something online just because everyone else was. At the moment, it feels good—but when your bank account takes a hit and your long-term goals get pushed aside, the regret hits harder than the splurge.

Financial FOMO usually starts with comparisons. You see what others are doing, and suddenly, your goals feel slow or boring. It's easy to forget that what you see online is just the highlight reel— not the full story. Some people might be using credit cards or going into debt to maintain that image. So, how do you fight the urge to keep up?

Start by practicing mindful spending. Before making a purchase, pause and ask yourself:

- Do I actually want or need this?
- Will it still matter to me next week?
- Does it help or hurt the goals I've set for myself?

Set personal limits ahead of time for fun spending. That way, you're not making decisions based on emotion in the moment. And when friends invite you to something that's outside your budget? It's okay to say no—or suggest a free alternative.

Real Talk: Two Teens Who Focused on the Long Game

Let's look at Bethany, who skipped out on some social outings to save for her own car. She packed lunches instead of eating out, picked up weekend shifts, and skipped a few online sales. Months later, she had enough to buy a reliable used car that gave her freedom and cut down her long, exhausting bus rides. Now her friends ask her for rides—and money advice.

Then there's Marcus, who turned down a brand-new gaming console and enrolled in a digital design course instead. He started freelancing on the side, and by the end of the school year, he'd made enough to buy the console— and saved extra. More importantly, he gained a skill that could turn into a career.

Both made short-term sacrifices for long-term wins—and they don't regret it.

But what about money anxiety?

FOMO isn't the only thing messing with your finances. Sometimes, it's just stress—worrying you'll never have enough or not knowing where to start. Financial anxiety shows up in different ways. You might feel stuck, avoid checking your account, or panic about bills and unexpected costs. That stress doesn't just stay in your wallet—it can affect your sleep, focus, and mood. Some people try to numb the stress by spending, while others freeze and do nothing, hoping things will somehow fix themselves (Mental Health & Money Advice n.d.).

Here's how to get a grip on that stress:

- **Build a Tiny Emergency Fund:** Even $100 saved in a separate account can give you peace of mind, knowing you've got something to fall back on.
- **Start Small and Simple:** A lot of anxiety comes from feeling overwhelmed. So break it down. Make one small money goal. Track one spending habit. Watch one YouTube video about saving or budgeting.
- **Talk It Out:** Talk to a trusted adult, mentor, or even a friend. You might be surprised how many people feel the same way. Having someone to bounce ideas off can help you think clearly.
- **Try Calming Your Brain:** Meditation, journaling, going for a walk, or even just breathing deeply for a minute can help settle the nerves when the money stress starts creeping in (Better Money Habits n.d., Robinson 2024).

Financial stress and FOMO hit almost everyone at some point. But every time you choose to slow down, make a smart decision, or plan ahead, you're building resilience—and that's way more powerful than any impulse buy. In other words, your money mindset doesn't have to be perfect—it just has to be growing.

MORE THAN MONEY—LIVING WITH INTENTION

Just like money anxiety and Financial FOMO, your money mindset is also shaped by the choices you make when no one's watching. Are you buying things because they truly bring you value or because you feel like you should? Are you always chasing the next thing, or are you pausing to appreciate what you already have? Let's dig into what it means to live intentionally—and how living simply, practicing gratitude, and giving back can change the way you approach your finances (and your life).

Frugal Living Isn't Boring—It's Smart

Being frugal doesn't mean being cheap—it means being thoughtful about your spending. It's skipping the overpriced coffee you didn't really want anyway, so you can put that $6 toward something that matters to you—like your first car or concert tickets you'll actually remember. Frugal living is about choosing value over trends. That could mean shopping secondhand, doing DIY gifts, or swapping clothes with friends instead of spending all your savings on fast fashion. It's about making your money work harder— not just harder for you, but for your future.

Example: Jalen decided to start bringing lunch to school instead of eating out every day. He saved more than $25 a week—money that added up to enough for a summer road trip with friends. His friends still hung out at lunch, and nobody cared about what he was eating. It turns out the memories were worth way more than a few takeout burgers.

Gratitude Is a Money Superpower

You might not expect the word "gratitude" to show up in a money book—but it's one of the strongest tools out there. When you learn to appreciate what you already have, you're less likely to chase things you don't need.

Take a moment each day to name one thing you're thankful for— big or small. A steady job, a meal you enjoyed, a friend who checked in, a pair of shoes that lasted longer than you thought they would. This kind of mindset doesn't just help you save—it helps you feel more grounded and confident in your choices. Gratitude also helps when you're working toward a goal. Instead of feeling like you're missing out, you feel proud of what you're building. That shift can help reduce spending driven by stress or comparison.

Volunteering: The Value of Giving Your Time

Sometimes, the best way to feel financially empowered is to give— not cash, but your time, skills, or energy. Volunteering connects you with your community, builds experience for your résumé, and teaches you to see value in non-material ways. You might help organize a fundraiser, tutor younger students, or serve meals at a shelter. All of those things remind you that money is a tool—not the goal.
Example: When Cherry volunteered at her local food bank, she learned how far a single donation could stretch. It made her rethink how she shopped and inspired her to start a weekly "nospend day" where she focused on giving instead of getting.

MONEY SMARTS CHALLENGE: MIND OVER MONEY

Let's pull it all together. This chapter touched on everything from goalsetting to handling money anxiety, dealing with FOMO, and finding meaning in how you live and spend.

Now, take a few minutes to reflect and answer these questions honestly in a journal, phone note, or private doc:

- What's one financial goal you care about deeply—and why does it matter to you?
- Think about the last time you spent money you didn't plan to. What triggered that choice? Would you handle it differently next time?
- When do you feel most confident with how you handle your money—and when do you feel stressed out by it? How do you
- currently define "success" with money? Has that changed after reading this chapter?
-

What's one simple habit you could try this week to lower stress, stay focused on your goals, or spend more intentionally?

Where in your life could you embrace more gratitude—or give back without spending a dime?

No one needs to see your answers, but writing them down can give you clarity, confidence, and a stronger mindset to keep making smart money choices that feel true to you.

You've taken time to look inward—setting goals, tackling stress, and building a healthier mindset around money. But there's one piece of the puzzle we haven't touched yet: other people. Because no matter how organized your budget is or how confident you feel about your savings, money doesn't exist in a bubble. You'll have to talk about it with other people. In the next chapter, we'll talk about communication and financial relationships—how to bring up money without it getting weird.

8

COMMUNICATION AND FINANCIAL REL ATIONSHIPS

You're sitting at the table, maybe after dinner, thinking about how to bring up something important—money. It might feel awkward at first. Maybe you don't know where to start, or maybe your family doesn't usually talk about finances openly. But learning to have conversations about money, especially with the people closest to you, is one of the most valuable skills you can build.

TALKING MONEY WITH THE PEOPLE WHO MATTER

Money talks with your parents—or any trusted adults—can help everyone understand what's needed, what's possible, and how to plan ahead. From figuring out how to save for college to working out how to manage shared costs at home, open communication helps avoid confusion and builds trust. ***Starting the Conversation***

You don't need a perfect script to start a money conversation. Just begin small. You could ask about your monthly allowance or how to handle your own spending money. These everyday topics can naturally lead to bigger ones—like saving for a car, applying for scholarships, or discussing how your family handles bills.

Bringing up money doesn't have to be heavy or formal. Try finding a quiet time when everyone's relaxed—after dinner, during a weekend, or even on a walk. Avoid jumping into serious financial topics during stressful moments. Jotting down your thoughts ahead of time helps, especially if you're nervous. Think of one or two things you want to ask or understand better, and let that guide your talk.

When Money Feels Like a Taboo

In some families, money is just not something people talk about openly. You might hear things like, "That's adult stuff," or feel unsure how to ask questions without seeming disrespectful. If that sounds familiar, try to acknowledge it in the conversation: "I know we don't usually talk about this, but I'd really like to learn and be more involved." Most adults appreciate honesty and maturity.

If the conversation gets tense, stay calm and respectful. Everyone has different views and experiences with money, and it helps to listen just as much as you talk. You don't need to solve every issue in one sitting. The goal is to start the dialogue—not to win an argument. ***Practice Makes It Easier***

If you're nervous about saying the wrong thing, try practicing ahead of time. Ask a friend or sibling to role-play as your parent so you can get comfortable with what you want to say. Or, write your thoughts down in a letter or message. Writing gives you time to sort through your thoughts clearly—and gives your family time to absorb your message without the pressure of responding on the spot.

Try This: Family Conversation Prep List

Here's a simple checklist you can create to help guide your next conversation at home:

- Choose a relaxed time when people aren't stressed or distracted.
  Write down two to three things you'd like to ask or share. Think
- through how to explain why this conversation matters to you.
- Be ready to listen—not just talk.
  Respect different opinions, even if you disagree. Follow up later
- with questions or ideas.
-
- By making financial conversations part of your regular life, you build stronger communication skills that will benefit you far beyond your family. It also helps you learn to handle money with more confidence—because you're not figuring it all out alone. The more you practice talking about finances, the easier it becomes. You'll be able to ask for advice, set goals together, and make better decisions with the people who care about your future.

PEER PRESSURE AND MONEY: STANDING YOUR GROUND

Let's say you're out with friends, and they suggest checking out that trendy new café where everything costs way more than what's in your wallet. You don't want to miss out, but your gut tells you the price tag isn't worth it. That's financial peer pressure. It's the kind of pressure that convinces you to spend money just to fit in or avoid being the odd one out. You want to feel included. And with social media constantly showing off other people's vacations, new shoes, and fancy meals, that pressure is everywhere. But giving in can pull you away from your goals and leave you wondering where all your money went.

Below are some tips to overcome financial peer pressure from friends:

Build a Budget That Works for You: A lot of people think budgets are boring or too limiting—but that's not the case. When you know where your money is going, you're the one calling the shots. Let your budget match your values. If saving for a car or college is your focus, your budget should reflect that. But you should still leave room for things that bring you joy—just in a way that won't throw your goals off track.

Practice Saying No Without Feeling Weird: It can be tough to speak up when your friends suggest something that's out of your budget. But setting financial boundaries is one of the smartest things you can do. Try saying something like, "I'd love to go, but I'm watching my spending right now," or "Can we do something that's a little less expensive this time?" You don't have to spill your entire financial situation. Just be honest and confident. The more you practice, the easier it gets. If your friends respect you, they'll respect your boundaries. If not, it might be time to rethink who you're spending time with. **Choose People Who Support Your Goals:** Surrounding yourself with people who have similar financial values matters. If you're serious about sticking to your goals, find friends who are on the same page. You don't need a big group—just a few people who support you and encourage smart decisions. You can even talk about money openly (without oversharing). Ask your friends how they budget, save, or avoid overspending. You might find helpful tips or even inspire someone else to take control of their finances, too. Remember, not all friendships are meant to last forever. If someone constantly pressures you to spend money or makes you feel bad about your choices, it's okay to step back. Your goals matter.

Watch Out for Emotional Spending: Sometimes spending is tied to how you feel. Maybe you spend more when you're stressed, bored, or just trying to keep up. One way to get ahead of this is to track your spending and how you felt when you made each purchase. Try keeping a spending journal. It doesn't have to be fancy—just jot down what you bought, how much it cost, and what was going on at the time (Discover n.d.).

At the end of the day, your money is yours. That means you get to decide how it's used. The more aware you are of your habits, triggers, and goals, the easier it is to resist the pressure to spend on things that don't serve you.

Peer pressure might be loud, but your goals are louder. They matter more.

MONEY SMARTS CHALLENGE: SPEAK UP, LEVEL UP

This challenge is all about building confidence in your money conversations—with family, friends, and even yourself.

Pick one of the prompts below and give it a try this week:

Start a financial conversation at home. It could be as simple as asking your parents how they budget for groceries or what their biggest money lesson was as a teen. Ask, listen, and learn.

Set a boundary with friends. If you're invited to something that's not in your budget, practice saying, "I'm saving for something important right now. Want to do [insert fun, cheaper idea] instead?"

Write a financial mission statement. In one or two sentences, describe what you want your money to do for you and why it matters. Example: "I'm saving for college because I want to graduate without drowning in debt." **Journal a money talk you want to have.** If there's a hard conversation you've been avoiding (with parents or friends), write out how you'd want it to go. What do you hope they'll understand? What outcome do you want? **Reflect on peer pressure.** Think about a time you spent money just to fit in. What would you do differently next time? How did it make you feel?

Remember: Healthy financial relationships start with honest conversations. Start small, stay kind, and speak with purpose.

Strong communication skills help you build healthy financial relationships—but even the best advice is only as good as the information behind it. If you want to make smart decisions, stay confident, and keep growing, you need access to reliable, up-to-date resources. That's where this next chapter comes in. From books and podcasts to apps and creators worth following, this is your goto guide for leveling up your financial knowledge—anytime, anywhere.

9

RESOURCES FOR CONTINUOUS LEARNING

Managing money isn't something you learn once and forget. It's a skill that grows with you—and lucky for you, there's no shortage of ways to keep getting better. From books and podcasts to YouTube channels
and creators worth following, here's your personal guide to leveling up your money smarts.

Must-Read Books

Books are timeless sources of knowledge. Below are some reads that offer powerful insights, real-life stories, and simple advice that sticks.

- *Rich Dad Poor Dad* by Robert Kiyosaki
    - A classic that flips everything you think you know about money. This book teaches you how to think like an investor, build assets, and understand the difference between things that earn you money (assets) and things that cost you money (liabilities). It's simple, smart, and still relevant today.
- *Your Money or Your Life* by Vicki Robin and Joe Dominguez This one gets
    - real about the link between money and happiness. It challenges you to rethink how you spend and shows you how every dollar connects to your time and energy. It's great if you want to stop living paycheck to paycheck and start making money work for your values.

- *The Richest Man* in Babylon by George S. Clason
    - Written in story form, this short book offers timeless money advice like "pay yourself first" and "avoid debt." Don't let the old-school language throw you off—it's full of solid, easy-to-remember lessons.
- *I Will Teach You to Be Rich* by Ramit Sethi
    - A straightforward guide packed with tips on saving, spending, investing, and automating your finances— without giving up everything you love. Ramit's style is casual and funny, which makes this feel more like advice from a friend than a lecture.
- *The Psychology of Money* by Morgan Housel
    - This one dives into why we do what we do with money. Instead of focusing on numbers, it focuses on behavior, decision-making, and emotions. If you want to understand your money mindset, this is a must.
- *The Latte Factor* by David Bach
    - This book shows how small daily choices (like skipping that fancy coffee) can add up big over time. It's not really about cutting lattes—it's about learning how habits can either drain or grow your wealth (The Finance Teacher n.d.).

Podcasts to Keep You Motivated

If you prefer learning on the go, podcasts are a great way to pick up new money tips while walking, commuting, or just chilling. These shows make personal finance feel like a conversation instead of a class.

- The Ramsey Show
    - Three short episodes a day filled with real people asking for help with real money problems. Hosted by Dave Ramsey, it's full of practical advice on saving, budgeting, and getting out of debt.
- The Clark Howard Podcast
    - Clark Howard shares smart money-saving tips, ways to avoid getting scammed, and tools to stretch your dollars further. It's great for staying financially sharp.

Women & Money with Suze Orman

Suze brings life and financial lessons together by focusing not just on the numbers, but on building confidence and a stronger money mindset.

So Money with Farnoosh Torabi

- This show features interviews with successful people from all kinds of backgrounds, plus tips you can use right now. Bonus: She answers listener questions every week.

- BiggerPockets Money
    - If you like hearing real stories about how people got out of debt, started saving, or hit big money goals, this one's for you. Every episode is packed with ideas you can borrow.
- AffordAnything with Paula Pant
    - This one's all about choosing wisely—because you can afford anything, but not everything. Paula chats with entrepreneurs and money experts to help you build a life you love (Dure 2025).

YouTube Channels Worth Subscribing To

YouTube has more than just entertainment—there are creators who break down money topics in fun, visual, and easy-to-understand ways. These channels are packed with advice you'll actually want to use.

- Debt-Free Millennials
    - Justine Nelson shares how she ditched $35k in student loans and built a life she loves—without huge income. Her advice is real, doable, and perfect for young adults looking to balance debt and goals.
- The Financial Diet

- This channel breaks money down into fun, digestible content. From budgeting hacks to lifestyle tips, it makes finance feel less scary and way more practical.

Graham Stephan

A real estate pro who shares everything he's learned about money, investing, and entrepreneurship. His videos also explain things like credit scores, saving strategies, and passive income.

- You Need A Budget (YNAB)
  - Want to budget better? This channel helps you set up a money plan that actually works. Short, simple videos teach you how to stretch your money and hit your savings goals.
- WhiteBoard Finance
  - Learn the ins and outs of investing, real estate, and starting a business. It's straight-talking content designed to help you build real wealth.
- Nate O'Brien
  - Minimalism, productivity, and money smarts all wrapped into one chill channel. Nate teaches you how to create a lifestyle that supports your financial goals— without overcomplicating things (Callahan 2024).

Influencers Who Make Money Smart and Relatable

Not all financial advice has to come from textbooks. Below are some content creators who explain real-world money topics in fun, honest, and totally relatable ways—right from your social feed.

- Tori Dunlap (@herfirst100k)
  - Known for mixing financial tips with empowerment, Tori focuses on helping women become financially confident and independent—perfect for older teens starting to make big life decisions.
- Humphrey Yang (@humphreytalks)
  - His videos break down big topics into quick, fun clips. If you're confused about investing, budgeting, or saving, he's got a fast, clear explanation.
- Haley Sacks (@mrsdowjones)
  -

Haley blends pop culture with finance, teaching you how to manage your money while referencing everything from Taylor Swift to The Kardashians.

- Milan Singh (@milansinghhh)
  - Young, relatable, and full of practical advice on how to save, earn, and invest without feeling overwhelmed. His videos feel like advice from a financially savvy older brother.
- Nicole Victoria (@nobudgetbabe)
  - Nicole teaches you how to budget without being boring. She makes financial planning feel approachable.
- Delyanne Barros (@delyannethemoneycoach)
  - She makes tough money topics—like index funds and investing for the long term—easy to understand and apply. Her tips are empowering and beginner-friendly.
- Sahil Bloom (@sahilbloom)
  - Follow him for quick insights on building good habits, thinking smarter, and understanding how money decisions shape your future (Greenlight 2024).

MONEY SMARTS CHALLENGE: BUILD YOUR PERSONAL FINANCE LEARNING TOOLKIT

You've just explored tons of books, podcasts, channels, and tools that can help you level up your money game. Now it's time to choose what sticks.

- **Pick one book from the list.** Read the first chapter this week and write down something that surprises you or changes how you think.
- **Choose two creators who explain money clearly.** Watch or listen to one of their recent videos or episodes.
- **Subscribe to one podcast or YouTube channel.** Choose one that makes financial topics easy to understand, and commit to checking in weekly.

- **Start a "Money Tools" list in your phone or journal.** Use it to save helpful links, tips, and ideas you want to revisit later.

There's no perfect system—just tools that help you stay informed, make smart choices, and keep learning. This challenge is your first step toward building a money toolkit filled with resources to keep learning and growing.

Congratulations on reaching this far! But we're not done yet because knowledge only takes you so far—it's what you do with it that really counts. In the conclusion, we'll pull everything together and focus on turning these lessons into lasting action. It's time to talk about building a financial life that thrives. Let's wrap it up strong.

CONCLUSION

You've reached the end of this book—but really, this is just the beginning of your money story. Over the past chapters, you've learned how money works in the real world: how to build a budget, save with purpose, grow your cash through investing, and make smarter choices with credit. You've picked up tools that most people don't learn until they're adults—and some never learn at all.

Getting good with money isn't something that happens all at once. It's more like building muscle. The more you use it, the stronger it gets. Starting now, even with small actions, gives you a major advantage. The earlier you learn how to manage your money, the more freedom you'll have to chase your goals, take risks, and live on your terms.

You don't need to know everything right away, and you don't need to have it all figured out. What matters is staying curious, being consistent, and learning from your experiences. Saving a few dollars here and sticking to a spending plan there adds up. Soon, those smart choices start working in your favor, and your money begins to grow right alongside you.

There will be challenges. You might face pressure to spend, doubt your decisions, or feel like you're behind compared to others. That's totally okay. Everyone moves at their own pace. What makes a real difference is staying focused on what matters to you and adjusting when you need to. Review your goals, reflect on your habits, and keep making small steps forward. Those steps add up to big changes.

And here's something important: What you've learned has the power to impact the people around you as well. Share what you've picked up with friends, family, or younger siblings. Talk openly about money and help others feel confident with it, too. The more we learn and grow together, the stronger our communities become.

There's a lot of noise out there when it comes to money—quick tips, hot takes, and pressure to keep up. But now you've got something better: knowledge, practice, and a plan. And that puts you in control.

So take what you've learned, make it your own, and keep going. You're building something powerful—one smart choice at a time.

"You don't have to be great to start, but you have to start to be great."

— ZIG ZIGLAR (GARVENS 2013)

You've got everything you need to succeed. Now, go make it happen.

REFERENCES

American Express. n.d. "7 Factors to Consider When Comparing Credit Cards." https://www.americanexpress.com/en-us/credit-cards/credit-intel/creditcard-comparisonfactors/.

Anders, Max. n.d. "The Brain Requires Repetition to Change." *Max Anders*. https://www.maxanders.com/the-brain-requires-repetition-to-change/.

Arizona Central Credit Union. 2025. "Money-Saving Apps for Teens: Budgeting, Tracking, and More." *Arizona Central Credit Union.* November 20, 2023. https:// www.azcentralcu.org/blog/money-saving-apps-for-teens/

Bennett, Karen. 2022. "Choosing an Online Bank? Look for These Top 7 Things." *Bankrate,* July 22, 2022. https://www.bankrate.com/banking/how-to-chooseonline-bank/.

Better Money Habits. n.d. "6 Ways to Tackle Financial Stress." https://bettermoney habits.bankofamerica.com/en/debt/how-to-overcome-financial-problems.

Birt, Jamie. 2024. "10 Top Online Jobs and Side Hustles for Teens." *Indeed,* June 12, 2024. https://www.indeed.com/career-advice/finding-a-job/top-online-jobsfor-teens.

Borghesan, Kris. n.d. "Americans Are Struggling Financially: 13 Financial Statistics You Need to Know." *Savology*. https://savology.com/13-financial-statistics-youneed-to-know.

Bromberg, Michael. 2025. "Investing for Teens: What They Should Know." *Investopedia,* March 14, 2025. https://www.investopedia.com/investing-forteens-7111843.

Brooks, Miles. n.d. "The 12 Best Crypto News Websites in 2025." Coin Ledger. https://coinledger.io/tools/best-crypto-news-sites.

Butts, Mason. 2024. "Question of the Day: What Percent of Gen Zers Don't Have a Monthly Budget?" *NGPF*, January 28, 2024. https://www.ngpf.org/blog/ques tion-of-theday/question-of-the-day-what-percent-gen-zers-dont-have-amonthly-budget/.

Callahan, Caitlyn. 2024. "Best Finance YouTube Channels to Follow." *Credello,* January 5, 2024. https://www.credello.com/financial-resources/personalfinance/best-finance-youtubechannels/.

Cote, Joe. 2023. "What is a Student Loan and How Does It Work?" *SNHU,* October 16, 2023.

https://www.snhu.edu/about-us/newsroom/education/what-is-astudent-loan.

Christian, Rachel. 2024. "How to Invest as a Teenager." *Bankrate,* March 26, 2024. https://www.bankrate.com/investing/how-to-invest-as-teenager/.

Cruze, Rachel. 2025. "Understanding the Psychology of Money." *Ramsey Solutions,* March 4, 2025. https://www.ramseysolutions.com/budgeting/psychology-ofmoney.

David. n.d. "Thrifty Experiment: How This Couple Lived on Just $34 a Week." *Moneyning.* https://moneyning.com/frugality/extreme-frugality/.

DeNicola, Louis. 2024. "Good Debt vs Bad Debt: What's the Difference?" *Experian,* September 13, 2024. https://www.experian.com/blogs/ask-experian/gooddebt-vs-bad-debt-whats-thedifference/#.

DeNicola, Louis. 2023. "What Is a Credit Utilization Rate?" *Experian,* November 5, 2023. https://www.experian.com/blogs/ask-experian/credit-education/scorebasics/creditutilization-rate/.

Dickler, Jessica. 2025. "Nearly Half of Credit Card Users Are Carrying Debt — It May Take Months, or Years, to Pay Off." *CNBC,* January 8, 2025. https://www.cnbc.com/2025/01/08/nearly-half-of-credit-card-users-are-carrying-debtreport-finds.html.

Discover. n.d. "Avoiding Financial Pressure." https://www.discover.com/studentloans/repayment/finance/financial-peer-pressure.

Downie, Ryan. 2024. "This Is the 8th Wonder of the World, According to Albert Einstein. And Utilizing It Correctly Can Help Make Saving for Retirement an Absolute Breeze." *Yahoo! Finance,* March 17, 2024. https://finance.yahoo.com/ news/8th-wonderworld-according-albert-202800026.html.

Dure, Elana. 2025. "Top 10 Personal Finance Podcasts." *Investopedia,* January 29, 2025. https://www.investopedia.com/top-10-personal-finance-podcasts5088034.

Egan, John. 2025. "Automatic Money-Saving Apps for the Forgetful." *U.S. News,* January 28, 2025. https://www.usnews.com/banking/articles/automaticmoney-saving-apps-for-theforgetful.

Fay, Bill. 2024. "Good Debt vs. Bad Debt." *Debt.org,* December 11, 2024. https://www.debt.org/advice/good-vs-bad/.

Federal Student Aid. n.d. "Student Loan Repayment." https://studentaid.gov/manageloans/repayment.

Fernando, Jason. 2024. "The Power of Compound Interest: Calculations and Examples." *Investopedia,* February 28, 2024. https://www.investopedia.com/terms/c/compoundinterest.asp.

Fidelity Smart Money. n.d. "What Is Zero-Based Budgeting and How Does It Work?" https://www.fidelity.com/learning-center/smart-money/zero-basedbudgeting.

First Commonwealth Federal Credit Union. n.d. "Financial Terms for Teens to

Know." https://www.firstcomcu.org/post/financial_terms_for_teens_to_know.html.

| REFERENCES

First Fed. n.d. "Basics of High-Yield Savings Accounts.". https://www.ourfirstfed.com/support/financial-education/basics-of-high-yield-savings-accounts.

Garvens, John. 2013. "You Don't Have to Be Great to Start." March 4, 2013. https://www.johngarvens.com/you-dont-have-to-be-great-to-start/.

Giovanetti, Erika. 2025. "7 Strategies to Get Out of Student Loan Debt." U.*S. News,* March 31, 2025. https://money.usnews.com/loans/student-loans/articles/meth ods-for-paying-offstudent-loan-debt.

Greater Nevada Credit Union. 2024. "Practicing Gratitude to Improve Financial Wellness." November 21, 2024. https://www.gncu.org/blog/practicing-grati tude-to-improve-financialwellness/.

Greenlight. 2024. "Top 7 Personal Finance Influencers for Teens to Follow." December 31, 2024.

https://greenlight.com/learning-center/saving/personalfinance-influencers-for-teens.

Hanson, Melanie. 2025. "Student Loan Debt Statistics." *Education Data Initiative,* March 16, 2025. https://educationdata.org/student-loan-debt-statistics.

Hayes, Mark. 2025. "23 Price Comparison Apps, Tools, and Websites (2025)." *Shopify,* February 2, 2025. https://www.shopify.com/ph/blog/7068398-10-bestcomparison-shopping-enginesto-increase-ecommerce-sales.

Hanson, Brad. 2024. "Budgeting for Teens: 18 Tips for Growing Your Money Young." *Credit Karma,* February 22, 2024. https://www.creditkarma.com/finan cial-planning/i/budgetingfor-teens.

Heid, Brandon. 2022. "Getting Started with Goal-based Financial Planning for All Life Stages." *eMoney Advisor,* December 21, 2022. https://emoneyadvisor.com/ blog/goal-basedfinancial-planning-for-all-life-stages/.

Helen. 2023. "How to Travel Smart: 15 Budget-Savvy Hacks." *Worldpackers,* June 22, 2023. https://www.worldpackers.com/articles/budget-savvy-hacks-to-travelsmarter.

Jacoby, Logan. 2025. "12 Most Popular Types of Cryptocurrency." *Bankrate,* March 28, 2025. https://www.bankrate.com/investing/types-of-cryptocurrency/.

Junior Achievement. n.d. "New Research Shows the Majority of Teens Feel Unprepared to Finance Their Futures." https://jausa.ja.org/news/pressreleases/new-research-shows-themajority-of-teens-feel-unprepared-tofinance-their-futures.

Laboure, Marion. n.d. "I Could Potentially See Bitcoin to Become the 21st Century Gold." *Deutsche Bank.* https://www.db.com/what-next/digital-disruption/ dossier-payments/icould-potentially-see-bitcoin-to-become-the-21stcentury-gold.

Lazarony, Lucy. 2025. "The Ultimate Checklist for Young Adults to Achieve Financial Success." *Investopedia*, March 14, 2025. https://www.investopedia. com/financial-tips-for-young-adults11678397.

Lee, Anne Marie. 2025. "Most Americans Can't Afford a $1,000 Emergency Expense, Report Finds." *CBS News*, January 23, 2025. https://www.cbsnews. com/news/saving-moneyemergency-expenses-2025/.

Lunas, Bernadette. 2024. "How to Get Started Investing for Teenagers." *InfoChoice,* August 16, 2024. https://www.infochoice.com.au/savings-accounts/great-longterm-investment-tipsfor-teenagers#Different-investment-options-for-teens.

Luthi, Ben. 2023. "8 Common Credit Mistakes and How to Avoid Them." *Experian,* July 5, 2023. https://www.experian.com/blogs/ask-experian/common-creditmistakes-to-avoid/.

Jessen, Jasmin. 2024. "Top 10: Ethical Investment Companies." *Sustainability Magazine,* October 29, 2024. https://sustainabilitymag.com/top10/top-10-ethi cal-investmentcompanies.

McNair, Kamaron. 2023." 22-year-old Who Lost $80,000 in Crypto: 'I Was Investing With

Money I Didn't Necessarily Have'." *CNBC,* September 7, 2023. https://www.cnbc.com/2023/09/07/22-year-olds-80000-dollar-crypto-losswhy-investingon-margin-is-risky.html.

Maher, Mackenzie. 2025. "Default and the Consequences of Late Student Loan Payments." *iGrad,* January 25, 2025. https://www.igrad.com/articles/conse quences-of-late-loanpayment-part-2-default.

Mastercard Services. n.d. "Digital Banking Innovations and Trends." https://www. mastercardservices.com/en/advisors/future-technology-consulting/insights/ digital-bankinginnovations-and-trends.

Matthews, Tyson. 2023. "Unmasking the Hidden Face of Greenwashing: How Businesses Can Be Deceptively Eco-Friendly." *Green Associates,* June 22, 2023. https://greenassociates.com.au/greenwashing-ethical-investments-how-tospot-them/.

Mental Health & Money Advice. n.d. "What Is Financial Anxiety?" https://www. mentalhealthandmoneyadvice.org/en/top-tips/what-is-financial-anxiety/.

MyPlate.gov. n.d. "Make a Plan." https://www.myplate.gov/eat-healthy/healthyeatingbudget/make-plan.

Newport Institute. n.d. "How Financial Stress Affects Young Adult Mental Health." https://www.newportinstitute.com/resources/mental-health/financial-stressmental-health/.

Robinson, Lawrence. 2024. "Coping With Financial Stress." *HelpGuide.org,* July 31, 2024. https://www.helpguide.org/mental-health/stress/coping-with-financialstress.

Schwahn, Lauren. 2025. "How to Budget Money: A Step-By-Step Guide."

NerdWallet, February 28, 2025. https://www.nerdwallet.com/article/finance/how-to-budget.

Schwahn, Lauren. 2024-a. "How to Set Financial Goals." *NerdWallet,* December 19, 2024. https://www.nerdwallet.com/article/finance/how-to-set-financial-goals.

Schwahn, Lauren. 2024-b. "Pay Yourself First: Reverse Budgeting Explained." *NerdWallet,* August 16, 2024. https://www.nerdwallet.com/article/finance/payyourself-first-reversebudgeting.

Schwartz, Marcus. 2024. "Digital Banking Statistics." *Superteam HQ,* December 18, 2024. https://www.superteamhq.com/post/digital-banking-statistics.

Snellgrove, Chris. n.d. "How to Build Credit as a Teenager." *EverFi.* https://everfi. com/blog/k12/build-credit-as-a-teenager/.

Spector, Nicole. 2023. "Nearly 1 in 3 Americans Don't Know Their Credit Score: Why You Should Check Yours." *Yahoo! Finance,* November 23, 2023. https:// finance.yahoo.com/news/nearly-1-3-americans-don-170002742.html.

Take Charge America. n.d. "5 Easy Ways to Avoid Financial FOMO." https://www. takechargeamerica.org/5-easy-ways-to-avoid-financial-fomo/.

TeenVestor. n.d. "How to Select Stocks." https://www.teenvestor.com/selecting-stock.

The Finance Teacher. n.d. "Top 7 Finance Books to Read in Your Teens." https:// thefinanceteacher.com/top-7-finance-books-to-read-in-your-teens/.

The Investopedia Team. 2024. "What Is a Credit Score? Definition, Factors, and Ways to Raise

It." *Investopedia,* September 20, 2024. https://www.investopedia. com/terms/c/credit_score.asp.
The Strategic Coach Team. n.d. "Mindset Matters: Abundance Mindset vs. Scarcity Mindset." *Strategic Coach.* https://www.strategiccoach.com/resources/the-multi plier-mindsetblog/scarcity-vs-abundance.
Thune, Kent. n.d. "Best ETFs for Young Investors: A Guide to Choosing Funds." *ETF.com.* https://www.etf.com/sections/etf-basics/best-etfs-young-investorsguide-choosing-funds.
Tippla. 2024. "The Benefits of Setting Up Automatic Savings Plans." September 12, 2024. https://www.tippla.com.au/finance/benefits-of-automatic-savings/.
Truist. n.d. "How Decision Fatigue Can Affect Your Mind and Wallet." https://www.truist.com/money-mindset/principles/mind-money-connection/deci sion-fatigue.
United Way of the National Capital Area. 2023. "Youth Financial Literacy: Why Is it Important?" June 6, 2023. https://unitedwaynca.org/blog/financial-literacy-foryouth/.
Valley First. n.d. "11 Ways to Stick to Your Budget and Jump Start Your Savings." https://www.valleyfirst.com/simple-advice/money/ways-to-stick-to-yourbudget.
Walk-Morris, Tatiana. 2023. "ICSC: 85% of Gen Z Says Social Media Impacts Purchase Decisions." *Retail Dive,* June 9, 2023. https://www.retaildive.com/ news/generation-zsocial-media-influence-shopping-behavior-purchasestiktok-instagram/652576/.
White, Jeff. 2024. "5 Micro Investing Apps to Consider." *SmartAsset,* September 25, 2024. https://smartasset.com/investing/micro-investing-apps-to-consider.
Yakal, Kathy. 2025. "The Best Personal Finance and Budgeting Apps for 2025." *PCMag,* March 7, 2025. https://www.pcmag.com/picks/the-best-personalfinance-services.

Printed in Dunstable, United Kingdom

72017885R00077